One Nation

Sergio Serna

Joker &
the Queen
PUBLISHING

ONE NATION

Disclaimer

This book is an independent work of fan-driven commentary and storytelling. It is not authorized by, affiliated with, or endorsed by the National Football League, the Las Vegas Raiders, or any of their associated entities.

All team names, player names, references to the NFL, and associated terms are used under principles of fair use for the purposes of cultural commentary, historical reference, and personal narrative. No trademark or copyright infringement is intended.

All opinions expressed are those of the author and contributors. Any likenesses, fan stories, or accounts of public figures are presented with respect and acknowledgment of their cultural impact. Where personal anecdotes are shared, names have been changed when necessary to respect privacy.

This book was written for the fans, by a fan—because some stories are too loud to be left untold.

Contents

ISBN: 979-8-9992221-0-7
Library of Congress Control Number: 2025912387

Cover design by Sergio Serna and Rachel Castro
Interior layout by Sergio Serna

Published by Joker & the Queen Publishing
San Jose, California

Printed in the United States of America
First Edition

For more information, contact: SergioLSerna@gmail.com

For the ones who stayed.
For the ones who never folded.
For the ones who bleed silver and black like it's a birthright.
For every heartbreak, tailgate, shady flag, and comeback.
For every "next season" that we rode out with loyalty and loud mouths.
For the folks who said, "It's just football"—
Nah. This is culture. This is bloodline. This is *One Nation*.
And to the Niner fans in my life—
You taught me patience, restraint, and the true meaning of keeping receipts.
You're the reason this book has spice.

Author's Note

This book isn't a timeline. It's a testimony. It doesn't follow a perfect arc, and that's on purpose. Raider stories don't live in clean chapters. They show up again and again, like a chant in the wind or a laugh across a tailgate.

You'll hear names come back. You'll see stories retold from different angles. That's not repetition. It's ritual. That's how memories work in the Nation.

Each echo is a tribute.
Each callback is a bond.
Each voice, each flame, each page is part of the same fire.

So don't read this like a playbook. Read it like a Sunday. Loud. Familiar. Full of family and feeling.
Because this isn't just a book.
It's our story. Told the only way we know how.
Together.

— Sergio Serna

Foreword: This Ain't Just About Football

I was born in the Midwest, where the rules were simple. You were either a Bears fan or a Packers fan. That was it. No middle ground. No straying outside the borders of that rivalry without catching heat. That was the culture. That was the line in the snow. But I never really fit into either camp.

Sure, I got caught up in the excitement of the Super Bowl Shuffle. Walter Payton was a legend, and you couldn't ignore his greatness. But even then, something in me felt disconnected. I could appreciate the talent. I could get swept up in the hype. But I couldn't feel it in my soul.

Because I wasn't built for pageantry. I wasn't wired for polite rivalries and structured cheers. I was born with an outlaw spirit. I needed a team that looked like rebels. Fighters. Misfits. Not choir boys in navy blue or cheeseheads with bratwurst in hand. I wanted edge. I wanted attitude. I wanted to feel something when I saw a uniform, not just nod along.

And then I saw it.

Super Bowl XVIII.

Marcus Allen was a machine that night. He was breaking ankles, reversing field like he had the remote control, and running like he had something to prove. The Raiders didn't just play. They dominated. The team looked like warriors. They wore black like it was war paint. Silver helmets gleamed under the lights like polished armor. And every time they hit someone, they meant it.

That was it. That was the moment. I was hooked. Instantly.

But it wasn't just the players. What really got me—what really stuck—was the crowd. The fans.

They didn't look like the tidy little families you saw on NFL commercials. They weren't country club types or families in matching polos talking about tax brackets and tee times. They looked like regular people. Like folks I knew. Folks who worked with their hands, who shouted at the TV, who lived and breathed and bled for something that made them feel bigger than their problems.

They were loud. They were proud. They were loyal and unapologetic.

And they repped Los Angeles.

That part mattered. Because at the time, I was still just a kid living outside of Chicago. California felt like another planet. Everything I saw about it on TV looked like a dream. Hollywood. Beverly Hills. The beach. Palm trees. People roller-skating in shorts in January. And now here was this team, decked in silver and black, repping that wild, sun-baked land with swagger and fury.

They had attitude. They had identity. They had *me*.

I didn't know if I'd ever get to see them in person. Unless they played the Bears or Packers, my chances felt slim. But I was already obsessed. I wore the colors. I learned the roster. I taped games on VHS. I was a Raider.

And then, just like that, life flipped the script.

My father got a new job. Suddenly, we were moving to California. I thought for sure we'd land in LA. I had my hopes up. But fate had a different plan. We landed in the Bay Area.

49ers territory.

That was a shock. The red and gold ran deep up there. Joe Montana was still royalty. Steve Young was warming up the throne. And those Niners fans? They didn't take kindly to anyone rocking black in their yard. It didn't matter, though. I didn't care. Because I was already loyal. I had my puffy Starter jacket, my Raiders hat, and my Marcus Allen jersey. I didn't walk in quiet.

Thankfully, the East Bay had its own army of Raider faithful. And that's exactly where we ended up living. It wasn't the Coliseum yet, but I was close. Closer than I had ever been. And then, like clockwork, fate stepped in again.

In 1995, the Raiders came back home to Oakland.

Destiny. That's the only word that fits.

The first time I saw them play live at the Coliseum, I went with my best friend Jr. and his family. We did it right. Parked at the BART station, tailgated like it was a religion, and then made the legendary walk across the bridge to the Coliseum. I'd done that walk for A's games before, but this was different. This was charged. This was heavy with meaning.

This was Raider football.

And then I saw it.

RAIDER NATION.

A sea of black. Some white sprinkled in, but let's keep it real—it was black. It looked like the stadium itself had decided to come to life. Grills were lit. You could smell carne asada and chicken wafting through the air like incense. People were dancing, laughing, playing music. There were fathers and sons, cousins and neighbors, complete strangers vibing like they'd known each other since childhood.

No politics. No drama. Just unity. Just family.

Some were tossing footballs across rows of parked cars. Others had little TVs set up to watch the early games. And it didn't feel like a tailgate. Not really. It felt like a reunion. It felt like home.

About an hour before kickoff, we started that walk. The bridge. The chants. The sound of drums, car horns, and fans talking smack to anyone not in black. I'd done that walk before, but I had never seen it like this. Thousands of fans marching together like it was a pilgrimage. It was alive. It was moving.

And yeah, I'm sure some visiting fans were there. But this story isn't about them.

When I stepped into the stadium and caught that first full glimpse of the field, it hit me. Hard.

This was a core memory. One of those forever moments you don't just remember. You relive it every time you close your eyes.

The wind hit my face. The smell of the grass floated up from the turf. The roar of the crowd pulsed through the seats. Even the damn seagulls circling overhead looked like they were ready to throw hands.

And then I saw them.

The Violator. Gorilla Rilla. The Black Hole in full force.

I wasn't just watching a football game.
I wasn't just supporting a team.
I had found my people. My tribe. My Nation.

Years later, that memory came full circle. I got to bring both of my children to a Raiders game. I stood next to them in the stands, silver and black on their backs, and watched their eyes light up the same way mine did decades earlier. That moment was bigger than any scoreboard. Bigger than any win.

I don't even remember if the Raiders won that day. I honestly couldn't tell you. I can tell you we didn't win a Super Bowl during that second run in Oakland. But it didn't matter. That's not what this has ever been about.
It's never just been about football.

It's about the Shield.

That pirate with the patch. That outlaw. That villain. The one who doesn't smile for the cameras but smirks when he knocks you down. The one who gets back up, every damn time, no matter what city he's in or what stadium they try to bury him in.

The Shield means something.
It means rebellion. It means pride. It means you've never needed permission to belong.
So when people ask me, why the Raiders? Why all this love for a team that's moved, lost, struggled?
I just smile.
Because if you have to ask, you'll never understand.

This is about the spirit. The culture. The community. It's about finding your people in a world that always tries to tell you to tone it down. And then deciding, proudly, to turn it up even louder.

From Oakland to LA. Back to Oakland. And now Vegas.

We ride.

We rep.

We bleed silver and black.

We are **One Nation.**

We are Raider Nation.

"What it means to be a Raider?"

*I*t means more than just wearing silver and black. It's about honoring the shield. It's about respecting every soul who ever bled for this tribe, every voice who ever screamed "RAAAI-IDERRRS" from the depths of their being.

This isn't just fandom—it's a chosen lifestyle. A way of life that's spanned the globe and run six generations deep. From back alleys in East LA to the sands of foreign battlefields, Raider Nation has always stood tall, unified by grit, pride, and purpose.

We don't just root for a team. We pledge allegiance to a legacy.

Renowned worldwide, we carry that commitment to excellence in everything we do. Loud. Proud. Unapologetic.

RAAAAAIDDDDERRS!!!! — *Violator, June 9, 2025*

1

Origins of Raider Nation

"The Autumn Wind is a Raider"
— from "The Autumn Wind," written by Steve Sabol, narrated by John Facenda

Raider Nation didn't just emerge. It erupted. Born not just from a football team, but from a rebellion, an identity, a statement. When the Oakland Raiders took the field in the 1960s, they didn't come with a clean-cut image or a polished public relations package. They came with grit. Swagger. A chip on their shoulder the size of the Bay Bridge.

The early years of the Raiders were chaotic. In fact, they didn't even begin in Oakland proper. The franchise's very first season in 1960 was played at Kezar Stadium in San Francisco's Golden Gate Park, a temporary home that felt borrowed and unfamiliar. The team was a mishmash of castoffs and dreamers, with modest expectations and little attention. But even then, a pulse could be felt. A sense that something wild and different was brewing.

The Raiders weren't even supposed to exist. When the American Football League launched in 1960, it had plans for a team in Minneapolis. That fell through when the Vikings chose to jump to the more established NFL instead. At the last minute, Oakland was awarded a franchise. It was rushed, underfunded, and without a proper stadium. The birth was messy, unplanned, and perfectly fitting for what this team would become.

For a moment, the team flirted with an identity that would've changed everything. They were almost called the "Oakland Señors." A misstep so glaring that even the city's most loyal fans rolled their eyes. That name didn't last. The Raiders did. The name that finally stuck felt earned, not assigned. Raiders sounded like pirates, like outlaws, like people you didn't want to mess with. It was aggressive, bold, and just rough enough around the edges to feel real.

Construction of the Oakland–Alameda County Coliseum began soon after. By 1966, the team finally moved into its true home. The Coliseum was raw and unpolished. An open-air concrete colossus tucked in the heart of the East Bay. It wasn't pretty. It didn't have the sleek design of newer stadiums or the historic charm of the older ones. But it had soul. It had noise. It had fans who were ready to make it sacred ground.

What emerged from those early, unstable days was something pure. A fanbase that didn't just support their team. They embodied it. The Raiders were more than a team. They were a movement. But to truly understand how this identity was forged, you have to look beyond the field. You have to look at Oakland in the 1960s.

The East Bay during that decade was a cauldron of upheaval, resilience, and reinvention. The Civil Rights Movement was at full volume. Oakland wasn't a quiet bystander. It was a frontline city. The birthplace of the Black Panther Party. A cultural and political revolution was unfolding just blocks away from the Coliseum. Marches filled the streets. Megaphones echoed through neighborhoods. Kids handed out leaflets while their parents stood in line for city council meetings. It was loud. It was raw. It was Oakland.

At the same time, the working-class backbone of the region was cracking. Industrial jobs were drying up. Racial tensions were high. The war in Vietnam cast a long shadow over every neighborhood. Families were struggling, but they weren't folding. Communities banded together—Black, Brown, white, immigrant, and Indigenous—and they found strength in solidarity. Strength in voice. Strength in defiance.

Oakland wasn't just another West Coast city. It was a firestorm. It didn't trust institutions. It trusted people. Your neighbor. Your barber. Your cousin who worked two jobs and still found time to coach Little League. That energy soaked into the DNA of the Raiders.

Al Davis saw it. He embraced it. He made it his blueprint. While other teams played it safe, the Raiders leaned into the chaos. Davis didn't build a brand. He built a culture. A football team that matched the temperature of its city.

These weren't your father's football heroes. These were warriors with sideburns, wild eyes, and a look that said, "We're coming for you." Al's "Just win, baby" attitude wasn't just about results. It was about defying expectation. These were people tired of being told to wait their turn. The Raiders gave them a flag to fly.

Silver and black wasn't a color scheme. It was a statement. A warning. A way of life.

You could feel it during the Raiders' first true home opener at the Coliseum on September 18, 1966. A 23 to 13 victory over the Kansas City Chiefs. It was physical. Quarterback Tom Flores threw for over 200 yards. The game set the tone. The East Bay's own "Mad Bomber," Daryle Lamonica, would join the following year and turn the deep ball into a weapon of mass disruption. On defense, Ben Davidson looked like a movie villain with shoulder pads, stalking quarterbacks with wild eyes and a handlebar mustache that curled with menace. These weren't just athletes. They were icons.

And above it all stood Al Davis. Already reshaping the game from the sidelines. Before he owned the team. Before the championships. Before the wars with the league. He had a vision.

The First Spark: Al's Origin Story

Al Davis was just 33 when he stepped into the spotlight. A young coach with no money but absolute conviction. He rolled into meetings with a film projector in hand and a hunger to disrupt everything. While other franchises played politics, Davis recruited overlooked talent from historically Black colleges and tiny backwater programs. He wasn't just building a team. He was building a philosophy.

When he took over as head coach and GM in 1963, Davis told the press, "We're not just going to play the game. We're going to change it." And he did.

Neighborhoods That Built the Nation

The love for the Raiders didn't just live inside the Coliseum. It lived in the neighborhoods. You couldn't walk ten blocks in the Deep East without spotting a Raiders flag waving over a rusted gate. San Leandro had Impalas painted black and silver months before the season opener. Fruitvale rocked Raider caps year-round, even in the heat. Richmond threw cookouts with extension cords running through open windows and TVs balanced on milk crates. Hayward's barbershops had Raider clips running in the background while fades were shaped and fades were debated.

The Nation wasn't confined to city limits. It stretched across the Bay. Fremont. Pittsburg. Daly City. Union City. Antioch. These weren't just fans. They were family.

Game Day, 1966

Before BART connected the region. Before Google Maps. Before parking passes and reserved rows. Getting to the Coliseum was a mission. A commitment. You had to want it.

Picture a father and son. Alfredo and twelve-year-old Julian. Their truck sputters into the lot, cooler in the back, folding chairs and pride stacked beside it. Alfredo's fingers still marked from a week at the plant. Julian's jacket stitched together by his mom from scraps of old uniforms and thrift store patches, each one black, silver, or both.

They step out into the smoke. The scent of ribs and charcoal thick in the air. Vendors push buttons and bootleg gear from behind card tables. Old Chevys bounce with bass. Somewhere, someone is already yelling about the refs and the game hasn't even started.

Inside, the Coliseum is alive. There's no luxury box, no cushiony seat, no reserved lounge. Just cold concrete and aluminum. And the kind of sound that hits you in your chest. Fans roar like it's war. Strangers become uncles. Touchdowns make grown men cry. For Alfredo, it's catharsis. For Julian, it's religion.

The Fan That Tatted the Shield

Frankie "Fresco" Ramos grew up in San Leandro. He owns Black Anchor Ink, a shop that's part barbershop, part museum, all heart. First Raider game? 1987. Bo Jackson went wild. Frankie never looked back.

Now he tattoos the Shield across the country. Arms. Legs. Necks. Even one guy's forehead. But the one that matters most?

"The Shield over the heart," Frankie says. "Because that's where it belongs."

Grandma's Gameday

Maria Elena Sanchez didn't miss a home game. She cooked pupusas and fried plátanos on a portable stove in Lot H. Her granddaughter Rosa, just seven, wore a glittery pink Raiders jersey. Some laughed. They stopped laughing when Maria Elena started calling out plays in Spanish before they happened.

"El blitz viene por la izquierda," she'd yell. Then—boom—sack. Everyone around her cheered like it was scripted. Rosa didn't just learn football in that lot. She learned pride. Generational, bilingual, fire-in-your-blood pride.

The Black Hole Before It Had a Name

Long before the Black Hole was formalized, certain corners of the Coliseum were different. Fans didn't just cheer. They performed. Full costumes. Face paint. Choreographed chants. They came for battle.

You didn't just walk into those sections. You earned it. You brought your loudest voice, your hardest clap, your best growl. And if you showed up soft, they'd let you know. Raider fans policed their own.

Rules of the Lot

Unspoken. Universal. Sacred.

- You eat only when the grillmaster says it's time.

- If we lose, you switch parking rows next time.

- First toast always goes to Al Davis. Doesn't matter what time it is.

- Don't bring your Niner cousin unless you want problems.

- Don't block the boombox with your folding chair.

- If someone hands you lumpia, that's your cousin now.

- Ice Cube lyrics are gospel.

- Clean your section before you leave.

- Only rival gear allowed is on fire.

- If the cops show up, you were already packing up.

The Soundtrack of Sundays

The music didn't stop. From 6:00 a.m. to kickoff, the Coliseum lots sounded like a live mixtape:

- Too $hort blasting "Freaky Tales"

- E-40 bringing Vallejo's bounce

- Metallica growling through 15-inch subwoofers

- Zapp & Roger pulling you into the groove

- Ice Cube laying down sermons of South Central and Raider gospel

- Santana's guitar weeping for the Bay

Each tailgate had its own DJ. Somehow, it all synced up. Like every block party you've ever wanted to crash.

Al Davis: Rebel. Visionary. Raider Forever.

Al didn't play by anyone's rules. He hired the first Black head coach, the first Latino starting quarterback, and the first female executive in the league. He sued the NFL when they tried to box him in. He wore white tracksuits like armor and moved his team like a king making war plans. Al didn't care what the world thought. He only cared about what came next.

He lit a fire in this fanbase. And even now, it still burns.

A Culture, Not a Campaign

There are good fanbases. There are great ones. But there is only one Nation.

You don't grow up a Raider fan. You're born into it. You inherit it. You protect it. And when it's your time, you pass it down. Like a story. Like a record. Like something holy.

The Autumn Wind doesn't fade. It waits. It finds a new voice in every generation. And when it does, you'll hear it, loud as ever, roaring through the smoke, silver and black against the sky.

2

Silver & Black Bloodlines

"You don't choose the Raiders. The Raiders choose you — usually before you're even out the womb."

The Shield Isn't Chosen—It's Inherited

There's a saying in Raider Nation that being a fan isn't a choice. It's passed down like a family name, or a sacred recipe. Maybe your grandfather whispered "Just Win, Baby" into your crib. Maybe your auntie wrapped you in a Raiders blanket before you could walk. Maybe it was your mom yelling at Jeff Hostetler in 1995 like he owed her money that sparked something in you. However it started, for many of us, this wasn't just a team—it was a birthright.

In homes across East Oakland, East L.A., South San Jose, Henderson, and neighborhoods without names but with all the pride in the world, Sundays were sacred. Not just because of church, but because of the other kind of religion: football, Silver and Black style. The smell of charcoal mingled with bacon and eggs if it was a morning game, or carne asada and grilled onions if it was later in the day. The hiss of a Modelo being cracked open. The voices of uncles debating Stabler versus Gannon while someone swore up and down that Derek Carr was just misunderstood.

It wasn't just a game. It was a ritual. It was church, therapy, and a family reunion all rolled into one.

Abuelitas in face paint. Tíos in shoulder pads and eye black. Kids learning how to yell "RAAAAAAAIIIDERS" before they could spell it. Dads handing down prized Bo Jackson jerseys like family heirlooms. Moms yelling louder than the TV commentary. There were no casuals in these homes—only lifers. Only bloodlines.

SUNDAYS WERE FOR THE SHIELD

Whole families would pile into beat-up SUVs and trucks, windows down, flags up. They'd drive hours to the Coliseum, to the L.A. Memorial, or to the cousin's house who had the biggest screen and the best grilling setup. These weren't parties. These were gatherings. These were bonds passed from one generation to the next.

Some kids grew up learning their ABCs from flashcards. Raider Nation kids learned them from jerseys.

"A is for Allen."

"B is for Brown."

"C is for Cortez Kennedy… yeah, he played for Seattle, but you better know him."

"D is for Davis."

"E is for Eric Allen."

"F is for Fargas, baby!"

Every family had that one uncle—war paint always at the ready, pinky ring too big, stories you weren't sure were real but didn't dare question. Every cousin had that first heartbreak—the moment they saw the refs hand the Patriots that game in the snow and learned life wasn't fair, especially not for the Silver and Black. That was our coming of age.

The Nation isn't just loud. It's layered. It's multigenerational. It's bilingual, trilingual, polycultural. Raider bloodlines don't run clean—they run gritty, passionate, and unbothered by what outsiders think. Because they're not supposed to understand. This isn't a fanbase. It's a family.

And in this family, you show up. Rain or shine. Win or lose. Oakland, L.A., or Vegas. The jersey might be black, but the loyalty? That's in the blood.

Rules of the House

Every Raider home had rules. Some written, most not. But all universally understood.

Rule #1: Don't talk during 3rd down.

Rule #2: Don't switch seats if we're winning.

Rule #3: If you cry when we lose, you're officially one of us.

In the Delgado household in Merced, the oldest daughter, Marisol, wasn't allowed to bring home a boyfriend unless he could name five Raiders from the '83 roster. One poor soul said "Joe Montana." He was escorted out before halftime. The family didn't even finish the wings he brought.

In a home in San Bernardino, every touchdown meant everyone had to high-five every single person in the house—including babies and the dog—or else the karma was off. Someone forgot one week. The team lost. They were exiled to watch the next game on a tablet in the garage.

Even the pets knew the game plan. Dogs named Bo, Maxx, or Renfrow. Cats named Woodson or Mad Max. One parrot in San Leandro that screamed "First down, Raiders!" at random intervals, even in the middle of the night. If it lived in the house, it knew the Shield.

Born into the Shield

You can spot someone raised in a Raider house without them saying a word.

– First Halloween costume? A toddler-sized Tim Brown, silver duct-taped "81" on a black hoodie.
– Baby photo? Raiders onesie, silver pacifier, attitude included.
– Prom outfit? Black dress, silver tie, Raiders clutch.
– Graduation cap? "RN4L" spelled in glitter glue.

For many of us, religion and Raiders weren't separate. Sunday morning service followed by kickoff. Communion, then kickoff. You asked for forgiveness during worship, then cussed out the refs by 1:15 PM.

The Story of Tito and Jacob

Jacob was eight when his abuela passed. The house got quieter, the tortillas a little less fluffy, the salsa less spicy. But his grandfather Tito stepped in.

Every Sunday became sacred. Same two chairs. Same blanket. Same AM radio playing the Spanish broadcast because Tito said it "just hit harder." Sometimes they muted the TV just to sync the voices. Before kickoff, Tito would nudge Jacob and say, "We don't just watch, mijo. We represent."

Touchdowns meant high fives. Interceptions led to bilingual cursing and slapping the table. That bond wasn't built on stats—it was carved into the soul. Tito's gone now. But every game day, Jacob still sets up that second chair. Same blanket. Same radio. That's how you keep legacy alive.

A Nation Without Borders

The thing about Raider Nation is that it's not tied to a zip code. You'll find us on military bases in Germany. In barbershops in Brooklyn. Taco trucks in El Paso. Swap meets in Yuma. We're global, and we've always been global—long before the NFL tried to be.

One fan from Albuquerque shared this at a Vegas rally:

"My tío never made it to a single game. Couldn't afford it. But every Sunday, he'd raise the Raiders flag on the front porch like it was the Fourth of July. Neighbors thought he was crazy. But when he passed? The whole block wore black that day."

That's the Nation. Sometimes loud, sometimes quiet, always present. Like a heartbeat. Like family.

Sisters in Sync

Cynthia stayed in South Central. Her sister Lani moved to Vegas. They don't see each other often, but every Sunday, they sync up via FaceTime—jerseys on, drinks poured, snacks locked in. The phones get propped next to TVs. They scream at the same refs in perfect harmony.

When Adams toe-tapped in the end zone? Cynthia screamed so loud the neighbor knocked on her door. When Crosby strip-sacked Mahomes, Lani dropped her phone, spilled her mimosa, and blamed the Wi-Fi.

Raider Nation doesn't care about distance. If you've got the Shield in your blood, you're never watching alone.

Coming of Age in the Nation

As kids grow, so does the fandom.

Raider birthdays turn into Raider quinceañeras, complete with black and silver dresses and a "Just Win Baby" backdrop for photos. High school portraits in Raiders jackets. Graduation caps with "RN4L" in rhinestones. Even wedding cakes topped with Raider helmets.

David from Antioch told us:

"My son was born during a Raiders game. I named him Jack, after Jack Tatum. The nurse asked if it was a family name. I said, 'You bet your ass it is.'"

Sometimes people grow up and move away. They marry someone from Kansas City or, worse, a Niners fan. They get jobs in towns where nobody cares. But that Shield still finds a way in—on their kid's backpack, on the car bumper, in the way they mutter "Damn refs" under their breath when a game's on in the background.

Heritage in the Details

Some families have crests. Raider families have cracked mugs that haven't been washed since the AFC title game. They have desk flags. Faded posters. Ticket stubs from '94. VHS tapes labeled "'89 MNF vs Denver." Shrines with candles. Maybe even a deflated football someone swears was used in an actual game.

One of the most powerful heirlooms? A voicemail from your dad that goes,
"I told you Carr was gonna ball out today, mijo. Call me back."

You never delete those.

Passing the Torch

Time is undefeated. And even Raider Nation has to say goodbye to its legends—on the field and in the family.

Uncle Manny's last game was December 2019. He had season tickets for 25 years. He passed away a month before the Vegas opener. His niece, Destiny, now wears his custom jersey with pride. The sleeves hang off her shoulders, but the spirit fits just right.

Julian, now in his twenties, still wears his father Alfredo's custom jersey to games. The lettering's faded. The sleeves are loose. But it smells like Sunday. It smells like home.

When asked why he still wears it, Julian didn't get poetic. He just said,

"It's his seat. I'm just filling it."

Closing Reflection: Bloodlines Never Die

You can change cities. You can change stadiums. You can even change quarterbacks. But you can't change legacy. You can't delete the imprint of growing up in a house where Raiders football meant family, meant pride, meant identity.

This fandom isn't a hobby. It's history. It's loud, it's loving, it's painful, it's funny. It's carne asada, cold beer, cracked remotes, and whispered prayers.

Because when you're born into the Nation, you're not just a fan.

You're a descendant.

3

The Battle of the Bay

"Like the great civil wars of the past... Batman v Superman, Iron Man v Captain America, Coke v Pepsi, those in the Bay also had to pick a side."
— *Sergio Serna*

LINES WERE DRAWN AT THE DINNER TABLE

Before we go any further in our journey through Raider Nation, we need to take a moment—just one chapter—to talk about the rivalry that split households, turned cousins into enemies, and made backyard BBQs feel like hostile territory. This isn't just another football feud. This is the Battle of the Bay, the most personal war in Raider history.

For decades, the San Francisco 49ers and the Oakland Raiders shared the same region but lived in completely different worlds. One side was bathed in red and gold, sipping wine in Montana jerseys. The other? Drenched in silver and black, flipping birds and blasting Ice Cube through sun-damaged speakers. It wasn't just football. It was culture. It was class. It was rebellion. And it was war.

This rivalry didn't need playoff implications. It didn't need division standings. It just needed a date and a kickoff. Because when the Raiders and Niners met—preseason, regular season, didn't matter—the Bay Area stopped what it was doing. Offices got quiet. Schools went tense. Homes divided like a Cold War border.

The first official meeting happened in 1970, but the tension had been brewing long before that. Two proud franchises trying to stake a claim on the soul of Northern California. Raiders fans believed they were the real Bay—gritty, street-tough, forged in Oakland concrete. Niners fans were seen as the polished side of the coin, country-club clean with khakis and Cabernet.

And on game days? It wasn't just stadiums that split. It was dinner tables. Aunties banned team colors from the house. Uncles refused to pass the stuffing to anyone in red and gold. Cousins didn't speak. Brothers slept in different rooms. Kids had to choose a side before they could tie their cleats.

Turf Wars at Home

We weren't just talking about a couple of jokes or trash talk. Real fights broke out. In the stands. In the garage. In the group chat. Allegiances were tested. Family BBQs were suddenly high-stakes summits. The Bay became a battleground, and no territory was neutral.

You knew what side a house was on by the flags flying out front—or the silence when you knocked. Some neighborhoods had Niners lawns next to Raiders driveways. You could tell who lost the last game based on who took their flag down. Some never did. Those were the lifers.

And those family gatherings? Half-sporting event, half-therapy session. Somebody was always one beer away from quoting Steve Young or showing off a Charles Woodson jersey like it was chainmail. Lines were drawn. And they weren't erased the next day.

The Scoreboard Never Settled It

By the time the final matchup came in 2018, the all-time regular season series between the teams stood at:

San Francisco 49ers: 7 wins
Oakland/Los Angeles Raiders: 7 wins

Dead even. A 7–7 split. No rubber match. No winner. No closure. Just two fanbases with scorecards etched in frustration.
Some of the most unforgettable clashes:

- 1970: The very first official game. Raiders 45, Niners 31. Statement made. The Silver and Black wasn't going to play little brother.

- 2000: Rich Gannon goes off for over 300 yards, Tim Brown catches fire, and the Raiders take it in overtime. Coliseum chaos. Fans stormed the aisles like we'd just won a playoff game.

- 2011: A preseason game so violent the NFL canceled all future preseason matchups. That's right—a preseason game. One where the parking lot tension bled into the bleachers. They called it off entirely. The NFL wanted no part of that smoke.

- 2018: The last dance. The Raiders got stomped, 34–3, but the fans didn't care. Raider Nation rolled deep. Loud. Proud.

Knowing this was goodbye. Not to the rivalry—but to the only regular-season outlet we had left to flex our pride.

Rivalry in the Blood

I didn't move to California until the mid-80s, but I learned quick. As soon as I touched down in San Jose, someone was already trying to convert me to red and gold. That glittery propaganda didn't stand a chance. I was Raiders for life. That "fool's gold" wasn't going to work on me.

Yeah, there's a photo floating around of me in a Niners jersey. That wasn't some crisis of identity. It was the result of a lost bet, and it haunted me for a week on social media. I got my revenge a few years later when those same folks had to rock the Silver and Black in public. Balance was restored. Family peace? Not so much.

I've seen Niners fans sneak into the Coliseum in disguise and Raider fans march through Levi's like it was a hostile takeover. Even if our squads weren't playing each other that year, the tension never left. The colors didn't fade. They stayed stitched to our souls.

When Jerry Crossed the Line

Nothing in this rivalry shook the Bay like the day Jerry Rice suited up for the Raiders. The face of the 49ers. The undisputed GOAT. Pulling on our jersey.

This wasn't some retirement tour. Jerry came to ball. He gave us nearly 3,300 yards and 18 touchdowns in Silver and Black. Every route was surgical. Every touchdown, a slap to the past. He didn't just play for us—he showed up for us.

For Raider fans, it felt like divine justice. For Niners fans, it felt like betrayal. Like Superman swapping capes. You don't just shake that off. The sight of Jerry wearing black still haunts some of them. We understand. That cut deep.

And he wasn't the only one.

- Ronnie Lott brought his punishing hits to our secondary.

- Charlie Garner crossed over and torched defenses in Silver and Black.

- Even Jim Plunkett had a red and gold chapter before finding his true destiny with the Raiders.

Every time it happened, it made someone's stomach turn and someone else's heart soar.

Raiders in Santa Clara?

Let's talk geography. The Niners play in Santa Clara. Not San Francisco. There are 40-plus miles between their stadium and the city on their jerseys. And this isn't a scenic route—it's a suburban slog.

Say what you want about the New York Jets playing in Jersey. That's across a river. This? This is like claiming Oakland while living in Tracy.

But sure—"Faithful to the Bay."

Meanwhile, the Raiders have moved cities, yes—but never lost the streets. Vegas might be our zip code now, but Oakland is still our heartbeat. LA still rocks our colors. And no matter where we roam, the Nation rides.

Culture Clash

This rivalry was always more than football. It was a cultural collision.

Raider Nation is fades, lowriders, soul food, metal horns, family BBQs, and black hoodies. We're carne asada smoke, Johnny Cash and Tupac, oldies and Ice Cube. We're the streets and the soundtrack.

Niners fans? They're Napa brunches, fleece vests, craft beer, and curated playlists. They're rooftop mimosas, Instagram filters, and designer dogs.

One side bleeds swagger. The other polishes it.

The Holiday Truce

Every mixed Raiders/Niners family has its own treaty system. Ours included:

- No team gear at Thanksgiving unless your squad won.

- No rewinding highlights during dessert.

- No trash talk for at least fifteen minutes after grace.

- If your team lost, you're on dish duty.

- Don't bring up Jerry Rice unless you're ready for a cold stare and a cold slice of pie.

Some families had to split holidays altogether. Thanksgiving at grandma's became two seatings—one for the Red & Gold, one for the Silver & Black. Neutral zones did not exist.

Bay Area Schoolyard Politics

Kids weren't immune. Playground politics got real. At recess, it was Silver and Black versus Red and Gold. You either ran with Gannon or cheered for Young. And if you switched sides mid-year? Canceled. Slandered. Written off like a busted fantasy pick.

Lunch table alliances formed. Trades were made—stickers for cards, cupcakes for loyalty. But once you picked? That was it. Your identity was locked in by second grade. Your side of the monkey bars was now enemy territory.

Even the lunch lady picked a side.

Street Loyalty and Barbershop Tension

Walk into any barbershop in Oakland or the surrounding areas, and you'd feel the divide. You might see a Jerry Rice photo on one wall and a Jack Tatum jersey framed right across from it. You start talking about "The Catch," and someone might nick your edge-up on purpose. Friendly fire? Maybe. But the message was clear: Watch your mouth.

Neighborhoods didn't just lean one way—they declared it. The East Bay repped the Raiders like it was blood. The Peninsula might've leaned Niners, but even there, you'd spot Raiders flags flapping from trucks, windows, and balconies. Pride didn't respect zip codes.

Tailgate Tales: BBQ & Beef

Tailgates for Raider games were already chaos—but when the Niners came to town? Whole different level. The lot transformed into a war zone disguised as a party.

One time, a guy in a Joe Montana jersey caught a full BBQ rib to the chest mid-argument. Not a beer. A rib. Dripping in sauce. The debate ended. Raiders run the Bay.

And these weren't frozen burger patties. This was carne asada, pollo asado, jalapeños on the grill, homemade salsa so hot it required a waiver. Ice chests full of Morelos, Modelo, Crown. Music bumping out of truck beds. You didn't need a ticket to feel the rivalry. Just a plate and a pulse.

A Classic Conversation

Niner Cousin: "We've got five rings."

Raider Uncle: "Cool. Can they help you find Levi's Stadium on a map?"

Niner Cousin: "At least we don't need a pirate costume to feel tough."

Raider Uncle: "You're right. You've got fleece vests and flat whites for that."

Niner Cousin: "Enjoy Vegas. That's your city now, right?"

Raider Uncle: "Always been our vibe. Bright lights, bold plays, and no wine spritzers in sight."

The Legacy

The Battle of the Bay wasn't about stats. It was about identity. It made holidays messier, tailgates louder, and Sundays unforgettable.

Even now, years removed from the last official game, the rivalry stays alive. In throwback jerseys. In group texts. In Instagram comments. In the side-eyes exchanged across living rooms during NFL Sundays.

So before we move forward, let's raise a glass to every cousin who stormed out of Thanksgiving. Every tia who made two types of nachos just to keep the peace. Every Raiders fan who stood their ground in enemy territory and kept it respectful—mostly.

Because once you're Silver and Black, you don't fold. You fight.

Welcome to the Battle of the Bay.

4

South Central to the Shield

"Just win, baby!" – *Al Davis*

When Al Davis uttered those now-immortal words, it wasn't just about football. It was a battle cry, a challenge, a philosophy soaked in swagger and sharp edges. Nowhere did that motto find a louder, prouder echo than in the streets of Los Angeles.

When the Raiders packed their bags and headed south in 1982, it wasn't just a change in zip code. It was a cultural eruption. L.A. didn't just welcome the Silver and Black. The city crowned them. From South Central to East L.A., from Baldwin Hills to Boyle Heights, the arrival of the Raiders felt less like a relocation and more like a resurrection.

The team didn't come to L.A. with white gloves on. They didn't ask permission. They dropped into the heart of the city and instantly mirrored everything about it. The chaos. The fight. The raw beauty.

The Coliseum Era Begins

The Los Angeles Memorial Coliseum was no ordinary sports venue. It was a concrete colossus surrounded by the sounds, struggles, and swagger of South Central. With sun-bleached arches and an open-bowl design, it had already seen Olympic triumphs, political protests, and cultural milestones. But once the Raiders moved in, the stadium took on a new identity.

You didn't simply enter the Coliseum. You stepped into something primal. It was hot, loud, and unfiltered. The bleachers were unforgiving. The sightlines weren't always ideal. The bathrooms were often disasters. None of that mattered. You came to rep your colors, not sip chardonnay in club seats.

Tailgates sparked before sunrise and raged long after the final whistle. You'd see carne asada grills glowing by 6:30 a.m. The streets buzzed with the low rumble of Impalas, Regals, and Cutlasses, trunks cracked open to blast Dre, Cube, and Zapp & Roger. Vendors hustled tees, tacos, buttons, and flags, some official, most knockoff. The whole vibe was unauthorized—and proud of it.

The Coliseum didn't promise comfort. It promised authenticity. And authenticity always wins in this city.

Oakland vs. L.A.—Different Temples, Same Religion

Oakland's Coliseum had its own identity—more brutal, more blue-collar, more "F you" in its bones. It didn't care if you were comfortable. It cared if you were loyal.

But L.A.? L.A. added style to the fight. Flair to the fire. The swagger born in Oakland found its echo in these streets, but L.A. wasn't trying to copy it. It made it its own.

While Oakland was concrete and defiance, L.A. was velvet rope and brass knuckles. The city's street culture shaped Raider identity in real time. Suddenly, the team didn't just look like rebels—they looked like kings.

A Team Becomes a Movement

From day one, the Raiders were embraced like royalty. Every part of the city wrapped the Shield into its identity. Logos appeared on classroom binders, garage doors, and backyard murals. Raider Nation wasn't just visible. It was embedded.

Kids who couldn't afford tickets still wore the hats. Teachers kept Raider bumper stickers on their desks. Preachers quoted Al Davis like scripture.

The team didn't just attract fans. It attracted culture.

Hollywood stars showed up in Silver and Black. Rappers repped the gear before they had gold records. College hoopers wore it on campus. MLB players threw on Raiders caps during batting practice.

In L.A., the Raiders weren't just a football team. They were a mirror. A movement. A manifesto.

The Kings Switch Colors—The Raider Effect Hits Hockey

In 1988, the Los Angeles Kings changed their colors from purple and gold to black and silver. That wasn't coincidence. That was cultural gravity. The Raiders made black and silver bigger than football.

The new look gave the Kings street appeal they had never known. Suddenly, kids who couldn't name a single hockey rule were rocking Kings hats and jerseys. Skaters wore them. Rappers wore them. Even punks and metalheads adopted the aesthetic.

The change wasn't about hockey. It was about tapping into the Raider energy—the outlaw cool, the no-apologies edge.

Raider Black Meets West Coast Rap

As West Coast rap exploded, the Raiders were right there in the spotlight.

N.W.A. didn't just wear the gear. They baptized it.

Dr. Dre. Eazy-E. Ice Cube.

These weren't football players. They were generals in a new kind of war. And their uniform was Raider Black.

Black hats. Black shades. Black tees. All wrapped around a don't-care attitude that looked a lot like what Al Davis had been pushing for years.

Raider gear became a street uniform.

It said something before you even spoke.

It told the world: I've seen things. I've done things. And I'm still standing.

Ice Cube said it straight: "The Raiders were the hardcore team, and we were the hardcore group. It was a natural fit."

He wasn't lying.

From the Streets to the Screens

The Raiders didn't just appear in rap videos. They took over the screen.

In *Boyz n the Hood*, Doughboy's cap told you everything you needed to know before he opened his mouth.

In *Menace II Society*, that Starter jacket flashed like a warning sign.

In *Friday*, Cube's Raiders hat felt like part of the dialogue.

These weren't wardrobe choices. They were cultural declarations.

Even outside film, the Shield stayed dominant.

Dr. Dre's "Nuthin' but a G Thang" made sure that hat got its close-up.

Kendrick Lamar nodded to the Shield in *m.A.A.d city* like it was passed down in his bloodline.

Eazy-E turned it into a legacy item—his look, his brand, his armor.

The Rise of Raider Streetwear

Snapbacks. Satin jackets. Pullover anoraks.
These weren't just fashion trends. They were symbols.

The handwritten script on the snapback? That was your crown.
The satin Starter zip-up? That was your armor.

The black Parka with the Shield stitched big across the back? That meant business.
You wore this gear with purpose.

These were the outfits that showed up in mugshots and magazine spreads.
They walked through high school hallways and parole board rooms.

They weren't clothes. They were declarations.

Street Art and Sacred Symbols

Drive through East L.A., Crenshaw, Compton, or Pacoima and the story was always the same.

The Shield was everywhere.

Painted on garage doors.

Tattooed on necks and forearms.

Airbrushed onto hoodies and jean jackets.

Laid gently next to candles at street memorials.

You'd see the Virgen de Guadalupe next to the Raider Shield—faith and fire, side by side.
You'd see Bo Jackson riding a lowrider, frozen mid-stiff arm, on a wall two blocks from a liquor store.
Even if you never played a down of football, the Raiders were part of your life.

Sidebar: Silver and Black on Screen

Boyz n the Hood — Doughboy's Raiders cap spoke louder than most characters.

Menace II Society — The jacket wasn't just cool, it was defiance woven into fabric.

Friday — The Shield sat on Cube's head like a family crest.

Music carried the message even further.

Dr. Dre — Made sure the Shield stayed in every frame.

Kendrick — Repped it like a neighborhood flag.

Ice Cube — Sharpened every lyric with Raider venom.

Eazy-E — Turned it into his uniform.

The First NFL Team to Look Like the City It Played In

This was deeper than branding. The Raiders were the first NFL team to truly reflect the culture of their city.

Other teams tried to appeal to their markets. The Raiders became theirs.

No NFL team had ever looked like this. No team had ever acted like this. And no city had ever claimed a team this hard, this fast.

A Fanbase Reborn in L.A.

The south stands at the Coliseum became battlegrounds. Chants ricocheted off the concrete. Homemade banners hung from rails. Airhorns and profanity rang in unison.

These weren't spectators. They were foot soldiers.

They didn't just cheer. They waged war from the bleachers.

Even after the team went back to Oakland in 1995, that fire never died.

The Rams might've returned later. The Chargers might've snuck in. But L.A. still bleeds Silver and Black.

The other teams have glitz. Have money. Have marketing.

The Raiders? The Raiders have the streets. They have history. They have scars.

And those don't fade.

Where It All Began for Me

This chapter ain't just history. It's personal. It's my baptism into Raider life.

It started with Howie Long—pure cement in shoulder pads. Then came Marcus Allen—silky as jazz but deadly as a razor.
And then there was Bo.

Bo Jackson didn't run. He erupted.

Bo didn't break tackles. He erased them.

He was myth and man all at once.

I had his posters. I studied his highlights like gospel. Sundays were holy, but only because they were Raider days.
That gear meant more than just being a fan.

It meant walking taller. Talking louder. Fighting longer.
This era didn't just shape my taste in football.

It shaped how I carried myself in a world that rarely gave second chances.
L.A. Raiders football didn't just make me a fan.

It made me family.

It made me Nation for life.

5

Our Most Hated: Rivalries and Refs

"They hate us 'cause they ain't us... and deep down, they wish they were. Too bad swagger ain't transferable." - Sergio Serna

Fan Story Disclaimer

These stories come from the realest corners of Raider Nation. Parking lots. Nosebleed seats. Blackout nights. Receipts that stretch longer than your cousin's bail record. Names and details have been changed, not to protect the innocent, but because some of you still owe us beers, bail money, or both.

If you think one of these stories is about you, it probably is. Stay petty. Stay loyal. Stay Raider.

If Raider Nation was built on pride, passion, and pain, then our rivalries were the fire that shaped the metal. They weren't just matchups. They were blood feuds. They carved out battle lines that stretched beyond the field and into identity. We don't just hate other teams. We remember why we hate them. That hate has names, faces, flags, and whistles. It's handed down like tradition and treated with the reverence of gospel.

The Kansas City Chiefs: Red Never Looked So Wrong

If the Raiders are pirates, the Chiefs are the navy. The ones in uniform, playing by the rules, pretending their tradition means more because it's dressed up in red.

Arrowhead's artificial noise and smug pregame rituals make Raider blood boil. It's not just the rivalry. It's the audacity. Ask any old-school fan about Lyle Alzado. Just the sight of that arrowhead turned him into a one-man wrecking crew.

And don't even bring up Rich Gannon. Our MVP. Our leader. Knocked out of the 2003 AFC Championship. That hit didn't just end a drive. It ended an era. The pain still echoes in our bones.

In 2019, Lot B fans staged a funeral for "Chiefs Kingdom." It wasn't a skit. It was therapy.

Fan Story: "Till Death Do Us Part—and the Chiefs Still Suck"

Darren and Carla Mendoza didn't want a church wedding. They wanted to get married where their love story started: the Oakland Coliseum. October 16, 2016. The day the Chiefs came to town.

The groom wore a black tux with silver lapels. The bride wore a jersey-stitched dress and carried black roses wrapped in Raiders bandanas. The officiant was dressed as a referee, complete with a yellow flag he used to eject two unsuspecting Chiefs fans who got too close.

Their wedding cake had Derek Carr on one tier and a crying Andy Reid topper on another. Their first dance? "Straight Outta Compton" remixed with Autumn Wind. Carla's tia fainted from tequila, someone grilled ribs in a smoker shaped like Arrowhead Stadium, and a Chiefs fan got ejected from the lot for saying "Mahomes is the future."

They say love is patient. Raider love is petty, proud, and permanent.

Fan Story: "Burial at Lot B"

In 2019, the Lot B Legends wheeled a black casket through the lot. Inside were a shredded Chiefs flag, a ketchup-stained Mahomes jersey, and a copy of Madden with a sticky note that read "Overrated."

The eulogy was delivered by "Reverend Raider X," who only spoke in Raider quotes and Tupac lyrics. "Somebody tell the Kingdom the war is over. We've claimed the throne."

Incense made from burned Arrowhead towels was lit. Red roses were thrown in. The chant "CHIEFS SUCK" was so loud, a news crew picked it up live.

One fan lit a sparkler indoors. He got detained. No one was mad.

The Receipts: Chiefs Edition

2003: No flag for the hit that wrecked Gannon.

2017: Phantom pass interference on fourth and long.

2022: Roughing the passer for landing "too hard" on Mahomes.

The Denver Broncos: The Mile High Mockery

The smugness hits different.

The Broncos act like they're above us. Like they're noble, while we're pirates. But make no mistake, that fake high ground is our playground.

Elway. Tebow. Manning. It doesn't matter who they trot out. The hate remains steady. So do the jokes.

Fan Story: "Bronco BBQ with a Side of Petty"

In 2004, a crew from San Leandro called themselves the Saddle Slashers. Their tailgate? A full-scale Bronco Buster BBQ.

They built a papier-mâché horse, painted it orange, drenched it in hot sauce, and roasted it while blasting Too $hort. Kids lassoed the fake horse with foam ropes. Adults were served chili in Broncos-themed cups, only to stomp them flat.

One guy wore cowboy gear. Underneath, a shirt that read "John Elway's Teeth Are Fake." Another held a sign reading "McDaniels is Just Hue Jackson in a Hat."

After the Raiders won, they passed out orange popsicles shaped like horse asses. That's how we heal.

Fan Story: "A Mile High in the Wrong Jersey"

In 2020, Anthony "Tone" Rivera showed up in Denver wearing a vintage Bo Jackson jersey. Beer was thrown. Words were yelled.

Tone didn't blink.

He stood up every time the Raiders scored and led chants from his row. At halftime, a vendor tried to charge him double for nachos. He paid with a Raider sticker.

Before leaving, he took a Sharpie and wrote "RAIDER NATION OWNS THIS ROW" on the seat. A kid asked if he'd come back next year.

Tone grinned. "If they don't ban me first."

The Receipts: Broncos Edition

1994: Phantom hold wipes out Tim Brown's game-winner.

2016: Roughing on Khalil Mack for light breathing.

2023: Defensive pass interference called on us for their pick play.

The New England Patriots: One Play, a Lifetime of Hate

The Tuck Rule didn't just steal a game. It shattered trust.

We remember the snow. We remember the fumble. We remember the lie.

Fan Story: "The Day I Quit Football (For a Week)"

January 19, 2002. Raul Torres from Hayward watched the Tuck Rule game. When the flag came out, he threw his remote into the TV. It was his first flat screen.

He burned his jersey in the backyard. Refused to watch the Super Bowl. His wife hid the car keys.

For a week, he wore only black and refused to talk about football. The following Sunday, he was back at the Raider Booster Club meeting, passing out rulebooks marked "Exhibit A."

Fan Story: "Tuck Rule Revenge"

When Chandler Jones stiff-armed Mac Jones in 2022, Sharon Contreras from East L.A. cried. Her dad had watched the original Tuck Rule game on a small TV in their garage.

He never got over it.

Sharon screamed so loud during the walk-off fumble return that her neighbor came running. She pointed at the screen. "It's finally even."

The next week, she got a tattoo of the final score, right under her "Family. Faith. Football." ink.

The Receipts: Patriots Edition

2002: Tuck Rule. Never forget.

2005: Holding called on a fourth-down sack. No contact.

2014: Helmet-to-helmet hit on Carr ignored. Picked off next play.

THE SEATTLE SEAHAWKS: THE EX THAT WON'T GO AWAY

They used to be in the family. AFC West. Twice a year. Fistfights and flinches. But just because they packed their bags and left doesn't mean we forgot.

The Seahawks were that annoying little brother—always trying to flex, never quite tough enough. Then one day, they caught a glow-up, got a Legion of Boom, and suddenly thought they ran something.

Old-school Raider heads remember when Largent got rocked. When Bo broke free. When the Kingdome felt like a haunted house lit in neon green. The rivalry might've faded from the schedule, but not from the memory.

Fan Story: "Coffee and Carnage"

In 2001, two Raiders fans from San Jose—Louie and "Big Pat"—took a road trip to Seattle in a busted, black spray-painted van they named *The Shieldmobile*. It had duct tape holding the bumper, a dangling skull on the antenna, and a boom box strapped in with bungee cords blasting Ice Cube all the way up I-5.

They pulled into the Kingdome parking lot six hours early, face paint on, Bo Jackson throwbacks crisp, and a sign that read, *"Coffee Ain't Strong Enough for This Smoke."* The sign had steam rising off it thanks to a portable fog machine rigged to a car battery.

Security gave them a look. A local threw a latte.

Big mistake.

Big Pat responded by holding up a giant cup labeled "TEARS OF SEAHAWKS FANS" and chugged it on camera. Local news picked it up and labeled them "Rowdy Raiders." A Seahawks fan tried to start something, but slipped on a patch of oil next to the Shieldmobile and faceplanted.

Security intervened before it turned into a full-on melee, but by the end of the game—a 27–17 Raiders win—the Shieldmobile rolled out of Seattle with two Raiders flags duct-taped to the roof, a cracked Seahawks beanie on the grill, and a fresh Sharpie message across the back window:

"Thanks for the coffee. Keep the L."

Years later, Big Pat turned that moment into a tattoo. The coffee cup, the score, and above it all: *"Seahawks Still Suck."*

THE PITTSBURGH STEELERS: PAIN IN THE SNOW

There's no sugarcoating this one. We hate them. They hate us. And it's pure, vintage, bone-deep football hate.

You can't mention the '70s without thinking of those bruising battles. We were the villains, they were the self-righteous. We had Snake, they had Bradshaw. We had Atkinson, they had Swann—and a whole lot of crying about hits.

Fan Story: "My Dad Punched a Terrible Towel"

In 1976, Freddy Gutierrez was a kid in Pittsburgh visiting family during winter break. His uncle—an unapologetic Steelers fan—handed him a Terrible Towel like it was sacred. Freddy used it to wipe his nose.
He got grounded. No TV. No dessert. No outside.

When Freddy got back home to East Oakland, he handed the towel to his father, who took one look at it and went full Raider mode. He stomped it flat while blasting "Boogie Nights" on vinyl, then punched it like it owed him money. The towel ended up framed in Freddy's garage with a plaque underneath: *"Some Fabric Deserves Violence."*

Years later, Freddy passed the towel down to his son like a war trophy. And when that son graduated high school, he wore silver and black under his gown, holding the towel during the ceremony. Every time a Steelers fan walks into their garage, they stop. Look. And walk right back out.

Fan Story: "Ice Bowl PTSD"

The Immaculate Deception still haunts us. Franco never caught that clean. We know it. They know it. Everyone knows it.

In 2022, a group of diehard Raider fans decided to spend Christmas Eve in Pittsburgh. It was freezing. One of them—Manuel "Mani" Chavez—brought a snow globe to the game. Inside was a mini Derek Carr, a Franco Harris action figure, and a custom label: *"Incomplete. Always Was."*

When TSA flagged the globe, Mani argued for 45 minutes. He explained the history. He referenced game tape. He quoted rulebooks.

They still confiscated it.

But the group didn't back down. During the game, they unveiled matching "Never Caught It" shirts and held up signs that read "Tuck Rule 1.0" every time the refs blew a call. After the game, Mani recreated the snow globe from scratch. It now lives in a Raiders bar in Fremont, placed in a glass case labeled *"Evidence Exhibit B."*

He returns every year on the game's anniversary to toast the memory of a catch that wasn't. To this day, he ends every sports argument with one phrase:

"If Franco caught that, then I'm Terry Bradshaw."

THE BALTIMORE RAVENS: THE FLOCK THAT FLOPPED

This one is newer, but no less bitter. It started with that 2000 AFC Championship. No Gannon, no points, no chance. That game was ugly—and unforgettable.

Ray Lewis got the glory, but Raider fans never forgot the elbows, the cheap shots, the flags that didn't fly. Every time we've faced them since, it's been with a chip on our shoulder and fire in our gut.

Fan Story: "Ravens Make Me Dry Heave"

In 2021, opening Monday Night Football in Vegas, Rudy Escobar and his daughter Angelina rolled into Allegiant hours before kickoff in matching "Ravens Ain't Real" shirts. The shirts were black with a purple cartoon bird mid-choke. Underneath it said: *"Just Choke, Baby."*

They set up shop in Lot J with a tailgate spread that included purple jello shots labeled "Lamar Tears," BBQ ribs dry-rubbed with a special mix called "Raven Dust," and a big-screen replaying the 2000 AFC Championship on loop—except it was edited to stop right before the second half. "No one needs to relive all that," Rudy said.

As the game rolled into overtime, Rudy paced like a man waiting on a baby to be born. When Derek Carr hit Zay Jones for the walk-off touchdown, Rudy dry heaved from pure stress and adrenaline. Angelina caught the whole thing on her phone. The clip showed him hunched over a folding chair, clutching a foam finger in one hand and pounding his chest with the other.

That video? It made it into their family group chat, their fantasy football league, and was even played on loop during Rudy's 50th birthday party. Every time someone brings up the Ravens, his wife just pulls out her phone and presses play.

They now call that moment: *"The Purge."*

Fan Story: "Welcome to the Wreckage"

After that same wild 2021 win, outside the loading zone at Allegiant, one Raider fan known only as "Vegas Dre" taped a cardboard sign to a Ravens tour bus that read:

"WELCOME TO THE DEATH STAR. BRING A MAP NEXT TIME."

The letters were drawn in silver Sharpie with little tombstones under each letter.

Dre had spent most of the fourth quarter with a sign that read "THE SHIELD STRIKES BACK." He wore a Darth Vader helmet with spikes drilled into it and carried a lightsaber painted like a Raider sword. A Ravens fan tried to clown him during the coin toss. Dre waited until the walk-off and then found that same fan outside the stadium and offered him a ride to the airport—with one condition: he had to wear a "Carr > Lamar" shirt the whole way.

The fan declined. Dre drove off slowly, honking the Imperial March.

Later that week, someone posted a photo of the sign still taped to the bus—now weathered, curling at the edges, but still there. That photo now hangs inside a Raider bar in Pahrump, right next to a signed picture of Tim Brown.

The Receipts: Ravens Edition

2000: Tony Siragusa body-slammed Gannon. No flag.

2015: Clear PI against Cooper. Ignored.

2021: Holding on Crosby not called in OT. Almost cost us the game.

The Los Angeles Chargers: No Rings, No Fans, No Respect

This isn't a rivalry. This is an interruption. A background character trying to get lines in the trailer.

Fan Story: "The Laugh Heard Round L.A."

In 2022, Julian "J-Dub" Rodriguez watched the "Tie That Never Was" in a Long Beach bar packed with Chargers fans.

When Carlson hit the game-winner, J-Dub stood on his chair and laughed. Loud. Disrespectful. Legendary.

"You begged for a tie. We gave you a boot."

When someone mentioned sportsmanship, he dumped ranch on their wing platter and walked out throwing double peace signs.
Banned from the bar. Viral online.

Fan Story: "Cigar Club"

After the 63–21 demolition in 2023, Marcus from Henderson lit a Cuban cigar inside Allegiant.

Security tried to shut it down. He pointed at the scoreboard. "That includes mercy."

He handed out business cards that read "Chargers Fan Recovery Hotline – 1-800-NO-RINGS."

One guy took six.

Marcus gave the unfinished cigar to a sad Chargers fan. "Might be the only smoke your team gets all season."

The Receipts: Chargers Edition

2010: Delay of game on us with one second left.

2016: Clear fumble recovery overturned.

2023: Touchdown ruled incomplete. Footage said otherwise.

The Referees: The Shadow Rival

Forget teams. Our longest-running feud is with the men in stripes.

They're the hidden enemy. The silent saboteurs.

We boo them like villains. We mock them like clowns. We track their names like bounty hunters.

Fan Story: "The Scales of Injustice"

In 2017, artist Maria De La Paz created "Lady Justice Raider." She wore a blindfold, a black robe covered in penalty flags, and carried a foam scale with a helmet on one side and a dollar sign on the other.

She passed out laminated "Official Bias Scorecards" before kickoff. When a call went sideways, she lifted her scale on camera. She went viral before the game even hit halftime.

Fan Story: "Index Card, My Ass"

After the infamous "Index Card" game, Reggie and his son started bringing a three-foot laminated card to every game. It read "Break in Case of Bullsh*t."

Eventually, it had lights and a siren.

By 2022, their section chanted "Check the Card" every time a ref got suspicious. One game, a ref laughed. Reggie didn't miss a beat. "Smile now, explain it later."

The Receipts: Stripes Edition

2002: Tuck Rule.

2017: Index Card.

2021: 14 penalties on us. Cowboys? Just four.

Top 5 Pettiest Raider Moments

1. Black Hole Wedding – Wedding party flipped off Chiefs fans in unison.

2. Just Win Echo Machine – Fan blasted Al Davis quotes through a megaphone at Chargers.

3. Day of Silence – Fans stayed quiet for one quarter after a league fine, then unleashed hell.

4. Bronco BBQ – Served chili in Broncos cups, stomped them flat.

5. Ref Candle Vigil – Sold out in 20 minutes. Memorial candles for "dead calls."

What It All Means

These rivalries didn't just teach us who we hated. They showed us who we are.

It's not just about football. It's about identity.

We show up. We plot revenge. We scream louder. We stay petty. We stay proud.

Raider Nation doesn't run from the fire.

We are the *fire.*

6

Sunday Is for the Nation

"Some teams have a home. The Raiders have a legacy that spans coasts, cities, and eras. We don't follow a map. We follow the shield."— Sergio Serna

Raider Nation doesn't just watch football. We live it.

We don't show up to spectate. We show up to represent. From the cracked pavement of Oakland's lots to the chrome-drenched tailgates in LA, to the neon-lit madness of Las Vegas, Raider gameday isn't an event. It's a calling.

This chapter is about more than kickoff. It's about the rituals, the rhythm, the flavor, and the fire that define each Raider city. We'll take you into the lots, onto the asphalt, through the music, meals, and madness that make Sunday sacred.

Three cities. Three stadiums. **One Nation.**

Oakland: The Grit

Night Before Gameday

Saturday night in the Town. You're prepping carne asada while the family debates whether Carr or Gannon had the better deep ball. You queue up NFL Network highlights from the 70s and 80s. Somebody's auntie is pressing tortillas. Somebody's uncle is making a liquor store run, always ending with a bottle of something brown and a 12-pack of tall cans. The garage has a Bo Jackson flag, a deep fryer, and a folding table already draped in black.

Gameday Diary (PST)

6:00 AM – The lots open early. You can smell it before you see it. Grills fire up. Generators hum. Chorizo sizzles next to eggs on cast iron. Fog curls low over the Coliseum. It's cold. It's damp. It's exactly right.

7:30 AM – Music kicks up. "You Dropped a Bomb on Me" by The Gap Band spills from a lifted Suburban. You toast with your neighbor, who might be your cousin or someone you just met. Doesn't matter. If they wear the Shield, they're family.

10:00 AM – Portable TVs show early East Coast games. Raider fans root against the Chiefs, Broncos, and Chargers with equal venom. Everyone's keeping score, even when we're not on the field yet.

12:15 PM – It's time. You fold the chairs. Flags get packed. A final shot of tequila is poured, usually by that one OG who's been tailgating since the sun was still hiding.

1:05 PM – Kickoff. You're on your feet. Maybe in the Black Hole. Maybe in the 300s. Doesn't matter. You yell until your voice cracks. You stomp until your legs go numb.

4:15 PM – Game ends. The walk back is either a celebration or a therapy session. But nobody leaves. You re-light the grill. Raider talk radio goes live. Tall cans crack open. You stay to dissect the play-calling, the refs, and every pass.

Inside the Coliseum

The bathrooms were broken. The lines were long. But the energy? Unmatched. Every third down was a test of vocal cords. Vendors knew your name. The PA system cut out half the time but nobody noticed—your section already knew what to chant.

Oakland Essentials

Songs

"Slippin' Into Darkness" – War

"Today Was a Good Day" – Ice Cube

"Computer Love" – Zapp & Roger

Meals

Burritos wrapped in foil, fresh from a last-minute taquería run

Lumpia straight out of your cousin's Tupperware

Chili verde slow-cooked in a Crockpot plugged into a generator

Rituals

Kiss the "Commitment to Excellence" sticker before your first drink

Light a candle for Al Davis before the anthem

Touch the infield dirt on the way to your seat if you sit low enough to reach it

The People

You'll meet the "Section Captain," the fan who's been in the same row since '94. The guy with a Bo Jackson tattoo and the kid he named "Al." Families who never miss a home game. Cousins who only speak during Raiders season. In Oakland, loyalty isn't a slogan. It's an inheritance.

Oakland wasn't fancy. It wasn't polished. It was raw, loud, and alive. The stadium was falling apart, but the soul of the Nation thrived in every crack of that concrete.

Los Angeles: The Flash

Night Before Gameday

South Central hums. Corners are alive with Raider flags flapping from street poles. Inside, families iron their jerseys, polish their jewelry, and rerun the Bo Jackson Tecmo Bowl clips like it's sacred cinema. Someone's blasting Tony! Toni! Toné! while marinating shrimp. Your cousin's cutting fade designs into his sideburns that end in double R's.

Gameday Diary (PST)

7:00 AM – Wake up to the smell of bacon and the bassline of Dr. Dre's "Let Me Ride." You grab a breakfast burrito and some Gatorade. Hydration and heat in one hand each.

8:30 AM – Pull into the Coliseum lot. Lowriders bounce past chrome tents. Some fans cruise in wearing silver shades, others post up early with portable grills and loudspeakers.

9:30 AM – The party's jumping. A local DJ has the speakers going. Someone's cousin is freestyling while wearing a "Just Win" chain. You dap up an OG in a throwback Marcus Allen jersey.

11:45 AM – Your final plate gets loaded. Lobster tail over jasmine rice. Mac and cheese that came from Grandma's house in a foil tray. Dessert is a plastic bag of homemade churros.

12:30 PM – You're inside. The Coliseum's sunlight hits hard. The Raiderettes are dancing. Fans flash double R's and chant like it's a playoff game.

1:05 PM – Kickoff. You yell so hard your sunglasses fall off. You stand. You sweat. You don't care.

4:15 PM – After the game, it's straight to Roscoe's. Or Crenshaw. Or Sunset. Raider Sunday never ends when the final whistle blows. It only shifts locations.

Inside the Coliseum

The architecture echoed. The sun roasted you. But nobody left their seat. Not even for halftime. The Coliseum had a bounce. A pulse. It wasn't just fans—it was a scene. And the Black and Silver were the stars.

LA Essentials

Songs

"Boyz-N-the-Hood" – Eazy-E

"Can't C Me" – 2Pac

"Let's Get Down" – Tony! Toni! Toné!

Meals

Tacos and carne asada fries with cotija

Soul food trays stacked with baked mac and hot links

Horchata poured into a gas station cup filled with ice

Rituals

Don't switch sides of the lot mid-tailgate. It's bad karma

Say "Bo Jackson" like a mantra before every home game

Light incense during the home opener while blasting "No Vaseline" for the ancestors

The People

You'll see custom grills. Raiders earrings the size of door knockers.

Families in matching jerseys. The fan who dressed like Suge Knight every game. LA Raider fans were hype, holy, and high-definition. They didn't just come to watch. They came to be seen.

LA Raider culture was street-smart, sun-drenched, and cinematic. Tailgates felt like block parties. Everyone dressed like they were about to be filmed. Style wasn't optional. It was mandatory.

Las Vegas: The Show

Night Before Gameday

Hotel rooms glow in silver light. Some fans light candles under mini helmets. Others double check bets on the sportsbook app. One crew's setting up a mobile bar in the trunk of a Dodge Durango. A family from Henderson watches old games with their kids and passes around a Raiders football signed by Tim Brown.

Gameday Diary (PST)

7:00 AM – Wake up in your hotel room. Maybe at The D. Maybe off the Strip. You check your fit. Jersey. Silver chain. Shades. Wristbands. Game face on.

8:30 AM – You hit the tailgate lot early. Raider Nation is already posted. San Diego car clubs. Sacramento flags. Some guy dressed as a silver Darth Vader.

9:30 AM – You grab food from the trucks. Tri-tip and slaw. Spam musubi with jalapeño aioli. Pineapple chunks on skewers. Banda blares from one side. DJ Mustard on the other.

12:00 PM – Time to enter Allegiant. Inside, it's pristine. Cool air. Black interiors. Feels like a luxury spaceship. But Raider Nation brings the fire.

1:05 PM – Kickoff. "Back in Black" rips through the speakers. The Torch lights up. The crowd goes from buzz to roar in five seconds flat.

4:15 PM – Postgame, you hit the Strip. Some fans go high-end. Others grab cheap beers at casino bars and argue about the secondary. Everyone's in black.

Inside Allegiant

You walk in and feel the future. AC pumping. Giant flame sculpture towering. More women's bathrooms than men's, because this stadium wasn't built just for guys. Raider Image is stocked with Oakland, LA, and Vegas gear—because we remember all our homes.

Vegas Essentials

Songs

"Back in Black" – AC/DC

"Still D.R.E." – Dr. Dre

"Tequila" – Banda Machos

Meals

Tri-tip sandwiches with jalapeño slaw

Deep-fried Oreos from roaming food trucks

Kalua pork sliders served hot off the griddle

Rituals

Bet the spread at the sportsbook. Always on the Raiders

One fan brings a black rose to every home opener. Nobody asks. Nobody stops him

Wear the same undershirt all season. Doesn't matter how hot it gets. It's for the team

The People

There's the fan who hasn't missed a game since 1988. The Vegas transplant who married into the Nation. The Instagram influencer who wears spiked shoulder pads and four-inch heels. It's diverse. It's loud. And it's still the Shield.

Las Vegas turned Raider gameday into a spectacle. But behind the LED flash and new-money polish was the same soul that once shouted from the East Bay bleachers. The same grit. The same pride.

Sidebar: Sunday Superstitions

You can't prove they work. But you can't risk stopping either.

Lucky Jersey Rule – If it worked once, don't wash it. That's how curses begin.

I Gotta Leave the Room Theory – You left, we scored. Now you leave every time.

Third Down Pose – Section 126 legend who stood three steps back on every third down. Never two. Never four.

Al's Shot – Every tailgate has a flask passed once with a whisper. "Just win, baby."

Silent Drive Curse – No one speaks during the first offensive drive. Not even for beer.

Pinch the ticket stub. Snap your fingers three times before the coin toss. Hum the Autumn Wind at halftime.
Some say it's silly. We say it's sacred.

One Nation. Three cities. One soul.

Whether it's a fog-soaked morning in Oakland, a sun-glare chant in the Coliseum, or a neon-backed bender in Vegas, the energy never shifts. It only evolves.
The cities changed. The stadiums changed. The seats, the signs, even the schedules. But the spirit stayed the same.

We don't follow a home team. We follow the shield.

Gameday is never just about the game. It's about the feeling. The pulse. The people.

And when the call goes out across the country...

RAAAIIDERRRSSS

We answer.

7

Homecoming and the Rise of the Black Hole

"Once a Raider, always a Raider."
— Charles Woodson, Pro Football Hall of Fame Induction Speech, 2021

The Return to Oakland (1995)

In 1995, the Raiders packed their iconic silver and black gear once again and made their way home. After over a decade basking in the glitz and grind of Los Angeles, they returned to the gritty, beating heart that first gave them life: Oakland.

Al Davis led the charge. Fueled by a relentless vision and a desire to restore the Raiders to their roots, he brought the team back not just as a business move, but as an act of legacy. It wasn't just about stadiums, money, or market value. This was about identity. About roots. About going back to where the blood first spilled.

Oakland welcomed the Raiders like a prodigal warrior. There were fireworks and parades, but more importantly, there was feeling. The kind of love that had no words, just a thunderous roar and a parking lot full of barbecue smoke. The people had never truly let go—and now, the Shield was back where it belonged.

The Coliseum underwent heavy renovations to meet NFL standards, most notably with the addition of "Mount Davis," a towering expansion of seats that reconfigured the stadium's face. Built through a controversial public-private partnership, it loomed like a concrete mountain over centerfield. Some fans hated it. Others tolerated it. But none of that mattered come Sunday.

Because while the view changed, the soul remained untouched.

This was still Raider ground.

Birth of the Black Hole

Even before the Raiders officially returned, something was already brewing in the shadows.

In 1994, while the team was still away, rumors of their return to Oakland gained momentum. And in that growing hope, a few diehards started cooking up a vision of what fandom could look like if the team came back. One of those fans was Rob Rivera.

Rivera wasn't just passionate. He was strategic. He looked at Cleveland's Dawg Pound and thought, "That's dope. But we can be louder. Meaner. Realer."

"This Dawg Pound thing... that is phenomenal," Rivera once said in an interview with *The Ringer*. "And our fans are better than that. We are bigger. We are better. We are badder. So if the team ever comes back to Oakland, why don't we do something like the Dawg Pound?"

He wasn't bluffing. He got to work.

By the 1996 season opener, Rivera and nineteen fellow believers had front-row seats in Section 105. They wore shirts emblazoned with "THE BLACK HOLE." They brought a life-sized dummy of the opposing quarterback and, in true Raider fashion, beat the hell out of it. It wasn't some PR stunt. This was ritual warfare.

And not everyone embraced it.

"It wasn't even kickoff yet," Rivera recalled. "Row 2 is like, 'Hey, man. Sit the f*** down!' Row 3, 'Sit the f*** down!' Throwing peanuts, water bottles, everything you can imagine. We locked arms and said, 'One sit down, we all got to sit down. One stand up, we all got to stand up.' And we did it, man. We did it."

That moment defined the Black Hole. Not just in its defiance, but in its unity.

The section quickly morphed into a madness-infused sanctuary of devotion. Rivera later described it like this: "They said, 'That is a good-ass atmosphere. That is a mosh pit.' So the mosh pit started to grow, grow, grow."

Game day became theater. Fans showed up decked in skull masks, face paint, spikes, armor, capes, leather, chains—whatever screamed allegiance and mayhem. It wasn't about dressing up. It was about transforming into warriors. It was spiritual.

When the Chiefs visited, Rivera and crew brought out a dummy labeled "Neil Smith," ripped off the face mask, and paraded it around like a trophy. When Ray Lewis came through, they swung his dummy while chanting "Mur-der-er" in eerie harmony.

And yet, through all that chaos, there was a mission.

"We've had to battle a negative stereotype of the Raider Nation," Rivera told *ESPN*. "If ever you wanted the best football fan experience, step into the Black Hole, because that's what we'll give you."

This was more than local.

The Black Hole went global. Chapters popped up in Mexico, Germany, Australia, and across the United States. Fans traveled thousands of miles just to stand in that section. To feel it. To become part of it.

Mark Acasio, aka Gorilla Rilla, put it like this: "His dream was that one day, with the blimp overhead looking down, the entire stadium would be the Black Hole. But the heartbeat would always be Section 105."

Radio host JT The Brick summed it up: "He is arguably the most important fan in Raiders history. There's a lot of guys who put on a costume, but Rob Rivera built it, grew it, and marketed it. He gave it life."

Iconic Moments and Legendary Games (1995–2019)

The Black Hole wasn't just noise. It was witness.

It watched Charles Woodson dominate and dazzle, bringing order to chaos. Tim Brown ran routes like poetry. Gannon fired lasers. Garner ran like he was mad at the earth. Wheatley bulldozed defenders. Romo brought tenacity. Janikowski bombed 60-yarders like it was nothing. Lechler pinned teams back into the Stone Age.

And through it all, Section 105 never blinked.

In 2011, just one day after Al Davis passed, the Raiders faced the Browns. It wasn't just another game. It was a spiritual gathering. The players wore their grief. The fans carried the weight. And when the Raiders pulled off the win, the roar from the Black Hole was like thunder echoing through the underworld.

Fans cried openly. Grown men hugged. Strangers clinked beers. It was more than a win. It was a tribute. Al's Torch hadn't been lit yet in Vegas, but in every fan's chest, it already burned.

Other legends rolled through in the twilight of their careers. Jerry Rice came in and earned true love. Warren Sapp brought his bark and his bite. Randy Moss flashed brilliance, even if things soured. Some showed up for the paycheck. Others stayed for the people.

And then there was Woodson. Again.

The farewell. The final walk. The fans chanting his name. It felt like royalty leaving the kingdom.

"You all mean the world to me," he said. And we believed him.

Challenges and Turbulent Times

It wasn't all glory.

The Coliseum aged badly. Pipes broke. Seats cracked. The infield dirt lingered until October. The franchise bounced between highs and humiliations. Coaches shuffled in and out. Management decisions sparked protests.

And yet, the Nation endured.

They stayed loud. They stayed proud. Even as relocation rumors to Carson surfaced, then Vegas solidified. Even as years passed without playoff wins. Even as media mocked them.

Raider Nation never flinched.

Prelude to Las Vegas: End of an Era

When the Vegas move became official, it cut deep.

Oakland had already lost the Warriors. The A's were threatening to follow. And now, the Raiders?

Fans raged. Protested. Held funerals in the parking lot. But when game day came, they still showed up. Still tailgated. Still sang the Autumn Wind.

The final home game in 2019 was heartbreak personified. The team lost, but the fans refused to leave. Some cried. Some drank. Some sat in silence.

It wasn't just an end. It was a goodbye to an era.

Legacy of the Black Hole and Oakland's Indelible Mark

The Black Hole became more than a section. It became myth.

In a league that tried to polish every rough edge, the Black Hole stayed defiant. It reminded people that football could still feel primal.

That energy carried to Vegas. Fans still dress up. Still chant. Still bleed. But they all know where it started.

Oakland was the crucible.

And the Black Hole? That was the flame.

You see it in murals. In tattoos. In kids who paint their faces because their parents once stood in Section 105. The spirit of the Black Hole didn't die. It scattered. It multiplied.

Allegiant may be the future. But Oakland was the soul.

As Al Davis said, "The greatness of the Raiders is in its future."

But the heartbeat? That still echoes from Section 105.
And it never stopped beating.

8

Don't Let the Ink Fool You

"The Raiders have always been more than a team—they're a family, a brotherhood that never breaks."
— Tim Brown, Hall of Fame Wide Receiver

The silver and black have always drawn attention. Sometimes it's admiration. Often, it's fear. And Raider Nation? We've been called every name in the book. Thugs. Outlaws. Criminals. Degenerates. The stereotype is loud and lazy, forged by media fear-mongering, sensationalist headlines, and yes, our own willingness to never tone it down for anyone.

But let's get something straight.

That story? It's not the full one. Not even close.

Because behind the war paint and spikes is one of the most loyal, generous, and misunderstood communities in all of sports. This chapter sets the record straight—bold, black, and undeniable.

More Than Meets the Eye

Yes, we look different. Raider fans show up draped in black leather, faces painted like warriors, chains swinging, skulls grinning, and grills flashing. We wear the vibe of rebellion on our sleeves. But it's more than a look. It's a message. A statement. We don't fit into the box, and we never asked to.

The league loves to call itself family-friendly. But to us, this is what family looks like.

Behind that face paint is a nurse who just finished a night shift. That guy in the Darth Raider helmet? He designs aerospace systems for a living. That woman in full black armor with spiked shoulder pads? She's a school principal who runs morning assemblies and after-school tutoring.

This is a fanbase filled with firefighters, nurses, city workers, veterans, small business owners, DJs, barbers, electricians, lawyers, chefs, and teachers. It's blue-collar and white-collar. Black, Brown, Asian, White, Polynesian, and every background you can name.

And the moment you put on that Shield, you're in. No background checks. No snobbery. Just love.

We don't care what block you're from or what tax bracket you sit in. You rep the Shield, you're family.

Community Over Chaos

The media clips want to show you a beer can flying or a scuffle in the stands. They don't show you what happens the other six days of the week. And they never show you what Raider Nation really stands for.

There are two groups that lead that charge—the Black Hole Booster Club and the Raider Nation for Life Foundation. These aren't slogans. They're structures built by fans for fans, serving people across cities, states, and even countries.

The Black Hole Booster Club: The Soul Beneath the Spikes

Founded by Rob Rivera in the 1990s, the Black Hole started as a vibe in the Coliseum's South End and grew into a full-on movement. What began with a few dozen fans dressed like villains turned into a global network with members in multiple countries and chapters in cities far from California.

They don't just show up on Sundays. They show up when schools need supplies. When families need food. When kids need toys, blood drives need donors, or shelters need volunteers.

The Black Hole has thrown barbecues for kids without fathers, held candlelight vigils for lost members of the Nation, and organized everything from scholarship funds to mental health outreach.
They wear leather and skulls, sure. But they lead with love.

"The world sees spikes and skulls. I see love, culture, family."
— Rob Rivera, Founder of The Black Hole

Today, there are chapters in New York, Arizona, Texas, Mexico, Germany, and beyond. Raider Nation isn't just mobile. It's intentional. And it keeps growing, not just because of loyalty, but because of legacy.

Raider Nation for Life Foundation (RN4L): Activating the Shield Within

Wayne "The Violator" Mabry didn't just wear the shield. He lived it. And with RN4L, he turned that energy into action.

What started as a passion project grew into a nonprofit that runs youth leadership programs, academic scholarships, military outreach, and anti-bullying initiatives. Wayne's mantra is clear: "You are the shield. Activate it."

That phrase is more than motivation. It's a blueprint.

Across schools in Nevada and Southern California, volunteers in Raiders gear lead workshops on discipline, emotional strength, and community values. They've helped teens get into college, secure trade school slots, and land first jobs. Not through handouts, but through hands-on mentorship.

"Being a Raider isn't about violence or chaos. It's about power—the kind that builds, not destroys."
— Wayne Mabry, The Violator

RN4L is now setting up chapters in Texas and the East Coast. And wherever the Nation travels, RN4L follows with purpose in hand.

Ink and Intellect: 5 Faces of the Nation

This fanbase isn't a cartoon. It's a canvas. Diverse. Sharp. Legendary. Here are just five names that speak to who we are—and how wide we stretch.

Tom Hanks – Concord, CA

Yes, that Tom Hanks. The two-time Oscar winner. The voice of Woody. The man behind Forrest Gump. Born and raised in the Bay, Hanks has repped the Raiders since the early days. He still defends the team when asked about relocations, saying, "Once you're a Raider, you're always a Raider."

Carlos Santana – San Francisco, CA

The guitar god with a soul full of rhythm. Santana has worn Raiders gear onstage, shouted them out mid-concert, and always leaned into the underdog. The spiritual energy of the Raiders fits perfectly with Santana's style—raw, fearless, and full of fire.

Dr. Richard A. Ornelas – San Jose, CA

An internist who treats everything from diabetes to hypertension, Dr. Ornelas runs his clinic like a commander. But between appointments, he'll break down game film or rant about missed coverages. A proud UC Irvine graduate, he's been a Raider fan since childhood and often ends his work week ready for kickoff.

Raider Greg – San Leandro, CA

The voice behind Raider Nation Podcast. Raider Greg has been holding it down since the early 2000s, providing passionate, honest, and sometimes brutally funny takes long before NFL social media got slick. His loyalty is loud. His insight is real. And for thousands of fans around the world, he's the voice that kept the Nation connected through every relocation and rebuild.

Gorilla Rilla – Las Vegas, NV

Born Joseph Salazar. Known to the Nation as Gorilla Rilla. He's been a fixture in the front rows since the 90s. Covered in silver chains, gorilla fur, and Raider pride, Gorilla Rilla isn't just a costume—he's a symbol. He shows up to schools, charity events, and fan meetups. His presence energizes. His purpose inspires.

"When people see the Gorilla, they smile. And if I can bring that energy—and represent what Raider Nation really stands for—then I've done my job."
— Gorilla Rilla

Raider Nation Worldwide

Raider Nation isn't just in Oakland, LA, or Vegas.

We're in Mexico, where Sunday tailgates are filled with tacos al pastor and choruses of "Autumn Wind" blaring from street speakers. Families show up three generations deep. Tattoos stretch across shoulders and backs. The love is generational.

We're in Germany, where NFL Europe sparked a fire that still burns. Cities like Berlin and Stuttgart now host Raider watch parties in bars and warehouses filled with smoke, flags, and Ice Cube tracks shaking the floor.
And now we're officially in Australia. The NFL designated the Raiders as the official team of the continent through its International Home Marketing program. In Sydney, Brisbane, and Perth, fans gather at sunrise to cheer in unison, wearing custom black and silver jerseys stitched with local slang and Raider shields.

"Even across oceans, the Raider spirit speaks. It's rebellion, it's pride, it's family."
— Suki Matsuda, Brisbane

No matter where you plant a flag, the Nation finds a way to fly it.

Trailblazers at the Top: The Shield Walked It Like It Talked It

The Raiders didn't just talk about diversity. They lived it.

In 1989, they hired **Art Shell**. First Black head coach in the modern NFL. Not an interim. Not a PR stunt. A leader. A Raider.

Before that, **Tom Flores** had already made history. The first Latino head coach to win a Super Bowl. And then he won another. His success wasn't accidental. It was revolutionary.

Amy Trask became the first female CEO in NFL history, earning the nickname "Princess of Darkness" for the fearless way she operated. She didn't just hold her own in boardrooms. She set the standard.

Then came **Sandra Douglass Morgan** in 2022, the NFL's first Black female team president. A lawyer. A regulator. A force. She didn't just make headlines—she made history.

"The Raiders have always stood for diversity, inclusion, and opportunity—long before it was fashionable."
— Amy Trask

These weren't token hires. They were trailblazers. And they came from the only team that truly walks the walk.

The Final Word

For too long, the world looked at Raider Nation and saw only the surface. The tattoos. The growls. The chaos. They forgot to look deeper.
But now, the truth is out.

We're more than fans. We're more than costumes. We're more than pain and penalties.

We are community. We are change. We are the living legacy of a team that never wanted to fit in, because we were always meant to stand out.

We are Black.

We are Brown.

We are loud.

We are loyal.

We are legendary.

We are Raider Nation.

9

Nomads No More

"The greatness of the Raiders lies in its future. And that greatness is you—Raider Nation."
Charles Woodson, Hall of Fame Speech, 2021

New Home, New City, Bright Lights-and Still the Raider Way

The story of the Raiders has never just been about the scoreboard. It has always been about the soul.

The people in the nosebleeds and the Black Hole. The ones who drove for hours to tailgate in the fog. The fans who painted their faces, flew across state lines, and tattooed the Shield over their hearts. The ones who stuck through decades of grit, heartbreak, relocation rumors, and rebuilds-never flinching, never folding, never walking away.

So when the team made the move to Las Vegas in 2020, it didn't just close a chapter. It opened a new one that came packed with tension, hope, and questions.

Oakland was our soul.

LA was our swagger.

Vegas? Vegas became our stage.

The Move Felt Like a Rebellion or a Funeral

Depending on who you ask, the move to Las Vegas felt like rebirth or betrayal. For some, it was a civic wound reopened. Another breakup. Another relocation. Another goodbye that felt unfinished.

For others, it was a clean slate. New energy. New blood. A second chance to build something fresh without forgetting where we came from.

Some fans walked away. Others leaned in harder.

That's the paradox of being a Raider. It's not supposed to be easy. It never has been. You don't fall in love with the Raiders because it's comfortable. You fall in love with them because it's real.

And when the Shield lit up in the desert, fans followed the glow.

Allegiant: The Death Star Beckons

Allegiant Stadium doesn't whisper. It looms.

Set off the Vegas Strip, jet black and massive, it looks like something out of a sci-fi flick. A monolith. A fortress. A Death Star. And while its curves may shine under desert stars, its purpose is rooted in Raider grit.

This stadium was built to impress, no doubt. But home isn't just steel and turf. It's chants echoing through concrete. It's smoke from carne asada rising in the lot. It's that first cold beer cracked with strangers who feel like cousins.

At first, Allegiant felt sterile. Too clean. Too corporate. Too quiet. Visiting fans flooded in. The building felt neutral. It didn't roar. It buzzed.

But Raider Nation doesn't stay quiet.

We adjusted. We adapted. We rebuilt the rhythm.

The chants got louder. The black got blacker. The lots got rowdy again. Slowly, brick by metaphorical brick, we made this place our own.

The Tailgates: Where Oakland Grit Meets Vegas Flash

Vegas tailgates are different-but they hit.

Out here, a lifted Silverado can sit beside a rented Bentley. Some folks are rocking beat-up jerseys held together with patches. Others show up in all-black suits with shoes too clean to be outside. You might see someone with a homemade Raider flag tied to their truck, posted up next to a group pouring micheladas out of five-gallon Gatorade jugs.

The smells are familiar. Birria. Brisket. Lumpia. Bacon-wrapped hot dogs. Tacos grilling over open flames. You'll find bounce houses for the kids. Silver-frosted cupcakes lined up on folding tables. DJs spinning Kendrick or Cube, while Banda or Bad Bunny competes from the next tent over.

And there's always someone with a tray of something homemade-empanadas, banana pudding, fried chicken. Whatever your flavor, it's here.

The lots don't come with rules. There's no "Lot B is for this" or "Lot C is for that." You park. You post. You rep. And if your flag says Raiders, you're good.

The vibe is familiar. It's Oakland, evolved. It's LA, reborn. It's Vegas, claimed.

Inside the Death Star

Allegiant isn't just sleek-it's intentional.

This is more than a stadium. It's a Raider cathedral.

From the moment you walk in, you're hit with a blend of luxury and legacy. Craft cocktails sit beside cold beer taps. Churros share menu space with nacho helmets. There's a DJ booth on one end and field-level suites on the other.

The sound system hits like a halftime speech from Al himself. The sightlines are perfect. And the air conditioning? Game-changer.

The building has more women's restrooms than men's. That didn't happen by accident. It happened because the Raiders knew who their fans were. Women have always rolled deep in the Nation. Allegiant acknowledged that with respect and action.

And then there's the Torch.

Standing 85 feet tall, the Al Davis Memorial Torch is more than a monument. It's the world's largest 3D-printed structure, assembled from aluminum and steel in over 170 custom-fabricated pieces. It glows from the core outwards, like a heartbeat. And when it lights up, the stadium pulses with it.

Near the Raider Image store inside, you'll find something small but powerful. Hats that read "Oakland Raiders." Others that say "Los Angeles Raiders." They aren't relics. They're respect.

The team knows its roots. They didn't erase them. They honored them.

Vegas may be the new home, but the past still walks these halls.

The Moments That Prove It

Vegas is still writing its story. But already, the moments stack up.

2020 – The home opener against the Saints. No fans, but a statement game.

2021 – Monday Night win over the Ravens in overtime. Chaos. Noise. Redemption.

2022 – The walk-off touchdown against New England. Chandler Jones. Lateral gone wrong. Insanity.

2023 – 63 to 21 over the Chargers. A beatdown. A clinic. A message.

2023 – The rise of Antonio Pierce. A coach with Raider DNA in his blood and defiance in his stare.

Each one stitched into the quilt of the Nation's new chapter.

The Shadow of Oakland

There's no sugarcoating it. The pain of the move hasn't vanished.

Some fans stayed in the Bay. Some never forgave. For many, the Coliseum wasn't just a stadium. It was sacred ground.

The cracked concrete. The faint scent of the infield dirt. The sea breeze. The history.

Allegiant can't replace it. And it doesn't have to.

Because when we moved, we didn't leave the soul behind. We carried it in car trunks and seatbacks. In playlists and patches. In every "RAAAIIDERRRSSS" shouted in a new zip code.

The culture didn't vanish. It adjusted.

Voices from the Nation

"It ain't the Town. But when you see black pour into the Strip, when you hear that first chant hit the roof-you feel it. This is ours now."

"I hated the move. But when I brought my daughter to her first game and saw her scream 'RAIDERS' next to strangers in full Black Hole gear? I got it."

"Vegas isn't a football city? Maybe not. But we are."

So What Now?

Allegiant isn't finished becoming home. Culture takes time. Ritual takes seasons. But Raider Nation doesn't wait. We build as we go.

The faces may look a little different. The backdrop has changed. But the edge, the energy, and the loyalty remain untouched.

We are still the fans who hug and growl in the same breath. We're still the ones who believe in underdogs, chaos, and miracles.

From cracked bleachers in Oakland to sun-drenched Sundays in LA to neon-lit nights in Vegas, the thread remains unbroken.

We don't follow a stadium. We follow a code.

That code is loyalty. That code is fight. That code is family.

A Glimpse of the Future

The future of the Raiders isn't vague. It's forming in real time. New stars are stepping up. Maxx Crosby, already a household name, has become the face of the franchise-a relentless force who embodies everything Raider Nation respects: toughness, passion, fire. He's not just a star on the field; he's a throwback to legends. To fans, Crosby feels like a modern-day Howie Long or Lyle Alzado-a warrior with attitude, a leader who doesn't just play like a Raider but lives like one. The way he hunts quarterbacks, rallies teammates, and speaks to the heart of the Nation? It's pure Silver and Black gospel.

The Raiders now boast a tight end duo that is turning heads across the league. Brock Bowers, the latest first-round pick and immediate starter, brings freakish athleticism, elite route-running, and a relentless motor that's already drawing comparisons to legends. He's the kind of matchup nightmare that shifts defensive game plans. Complementing him is Michael Mayer, who brings old-school toughness, smart blocking, and reliable hands. Together, they form a devastating one-two punch-a modern pairing that can line up anywhere, stretch the field, and punish defenses from multiple formations. One is the star. The other is the hammer. And both are pure Raider.

Tyree Wilson is rounding into the menace he was drafted to be, a disruptor off the edge who looks like he belongs next to Crosby on every down. And Jakorian Bennett? The kid is raw, but you can see the flashes. You can see what they saw on draft night.

This past season, the Raiders drafted Brock Bowers, an elite tight end with freakish athleticism and route running that's already drawing comparisons to legends. Pairing him with Mayer opens up new dimensions for the offense.

And in the latest draft, they added Ashton Jeanty-a back with power, burst, and vision that could anchor the run game for years to come.

Under center, the answer is shifting. The Raiders traded for Geno Smith, a veteran presence with poise, mobility, and something to prove. He brings leadership and a chip on his shoulder-two things Raider Nation always respects.

And overseeing it all is Pete Carroll. That's right. The silver-haired motivator who once ruled the NFC West with Seattle is now calling the shots for the Raiders. It's unexpected. It's unorthodox. And somehow, it fits.

His energy, championship pedigree, and ability to develop players is already turning heads. The locker room has bought in. The fanbase is watching with cautious optimism. Raider football, under Carroll, might not look traditional-but tradition in this franchise has always been about shaking the norm.

We may not know the exact shape of the next five years, but we know who we are. We fight. We rise. We rebuild. We wear black to every funeral and turn it into a celebration.

This isn't a goodbye to who we were. It's a continuation of who we've always been.

We're not lost. We're not guests. We're home.

And we're still...

One Nation.

10

My Raider Story

My Raider story isn't a chapter. It's the whole damn book.

This team could relocate to Mars, and I would still rep them. It doesn't matter if the field's made of red dust or turf. If the helmet's silver, if the jerseys are black, if that Shield is still gleaming like a middle finger to convention, I'm in. The Raiders aren't just a football team to me. They're a constant. A compass. A rebellion wrapped in fabric and stitched into my soul.

I think back to those early Sundays, when we'd rise with the sun. Six a.m., no complaints, just that familiar buzz in our bones. Me, Jr, Moi, Big Al, and the whole crew. We didn't need alarms. Raider Sunday was the alarm. We'd roll out, bleary-eyed but electric, heading straight for the BART parking lot. Everyone had a role. Someone brought the grill. Someone brought the speaker. Someone always forgot the bottle opener but remembered the salsa.

We weren't just tailgating. We were testifying.

It wasn't just football. It was ritual. Brotherhood. Smoke and soul and second chances. The laughter cracked like thunder through the morning chill. You could smell carne asada mixing with engine exhaust. Someone bumped "Slippin' Into Darkness," and we all nodded like it was gospel. These weren't just fans. These were my people.

Over time, that tribe didn't shrink. It multiplied.

Now, if I get the chance to roll to a game, I usually roll with mine. My son Jackson, my little warrior, the next chapter of this legacy. Watching him throw on that jersey, puff his chest out with pride, raise his arms after a big play—there's nothing like it. I see myself in his fire. That same stubborn loyalty. That same hunger for the underdog fight.

He's learning the rhythms now. The chants, the rituals, the heartbreaks. The beauty of it all is, he's not just watching a game. He's stepping into something sacred. Something passed down like vinyl records or handwritten recipes. That Shield on his chest isn't just a logo. It's lineage.

My wife, Rachel Castro, has her own story with this team. And it didn't start as a love story. She grew up a diehard A's fan. One of the real ones. And Mt. Davis? She hated it. Said it ruined the Coliseum's view of the East Oakland hills. She swore she'd never cheer for the Raiders, not while that concrete monster cast a shadow on her memories. I respected that. Pain is pain, no matter what colors you wear.

But life has a funny way of rewriting stories.

When the A's turned their backs on Oakland, when ownership gutted the heart of a loyal fanbase, Rachel saw what it felt like to be discarded. And then she saw how the Raiders, even after relocating, kept honoring their roots. They still stock Oakland gear at Allegiant. They still shout out the cities that built them. They never pretended the past didn't matter.

That made an impact. Her bitterness softened. And now? Let's just say there are more than a few pieces of Raiders clothing in her closet. I won't say Taylor Swift helped, but I won't say she didn't either.

And Rachel's Tía Marge? If you haven't partied with her before a Raiders game, you haven't lived. She's part historian, part hype woman, part tequila whisperer. I'd tailgate with her any day of the week, or every day if she's pouring.

My Raider circle goes wider still. My sister Patsy, always holding it down with love and fire. My niece Chanelle and her wife Mel, ride-or-die season ticket holders in Vegas who rep the Shield like it's stitched into their DNA. If there's a chant to scream or a flag to wave, they're already leading the way.

And then there's Uncle Fred. He grew up a Cowboys fan. But something happened in Vegas. Like the city itself, he made a switch. Maybe it was the style, maybe it was the passion, maybe it was just time. Whatever the reason, he and his son Julian are Raiders now. They wear the black. They rep the Nation. They started as a fictional father-son tribute in these pages. But believe me, they're real. Real fans. Real family.

Some days, I don't roll deep. Some days, I roll solo.

But the truth is, I'm never really alone.

This team has been the thread that runs through my life. From the smoke-choked lots of Oakland to the neon flash of Vegas, from late-night replays to Sunday morning setups, the Raiders have been my constant. My connection. My rhythm.

It's not about who's next to me in the seats anymore. It's about who's with me in spirit. Jr, Moi, Big Al. My late friend Becky, the one who told me I should write this book. She's still here. I feel her when the anthem plays. When the team takes the field. When the Shield rises and the crowd erupts like thunder.

This is legacy. This is bloodline.

Every grillmaster in Lot B. Every fan in the Black Hole. Every kid in a homemade jersey screaming at a TV in East San Jose. That's my family. That's our family.

I've got brothers in the 300s. Cousins in Section 126. Aunts in Vegas suites. Uncles running pop-up tents with bootleg merch and ice-cold Tecates. I've got Raider fans in Mexico, blasting Cube and Santana while tacos sizzle. I've got fans in Germany, setting alarms at 2 a.m. to watch the game in basements turned into mini Coliseums.

We span oceans, cities, and time zones. We don't follow maps. We follow the Shield.

The truth is, being a Raider doesn't start at kickoff and it doesn't end with the whistle. It's not seasonal. It's not convenient. It's not about the standings or the sportsbook odds.

It's about the feeling. The pride. The unity.

It's knowing that no matter where you are in the world, if you shout "RAIDERS," someone will echo it back.

Me? I've been all in since the first time I saw silver helmets glinting under the lights. Since I saw Bo break free. Since I saw a city rally around a team that didn't ask for permission to be great.

And when my time comes, I want to go out the same way I've lived. Draped in black. Smiling like I just watched Marcus Allen turn the corner. And with one last whisper to the heavens...RAAAAAIDERRRSSS.

Because I am a Raider... And we—we are Raider Nation.

My People. My Heart. My Thanks.

This book was a labor of love, and like all labors, it came with its share of pain. But before anything else, I dedicate it to Rachel. Without your unwavering support, patience, and love, none of this would have been possible. You manage our kids, a classroom full of other people's kids, and—on more occasions than I care to admit—me when I'm acting like a kid. You're a superhero in plain clothes, and I love you for it.

To my children, Jesse and Jax—this book is a part of me, and so are you. You are my reason. Every page, every story, every late-night writing session was fueled by love for you. I hope you grow up knowing that passion matters, that your voice deserves to be heard, and that being a fan, a dreamer, or even a little wild sometimes... can still lead to something beautiful. Being your dad is my greatest joy and proudest title.

To my sisters, Patsy and Lindsay—thank you for always having my back and keeping me grounded when life was anything but. And to my nieces and nephew, Chanelle, Elizabeth, Valoree, Kassidy, and Brandon—you each carry a spark that reminds me why family matters most. I'm proud to be your uncle.

Garrett, Emily, Mackenzie, and Jackson—being with Rachel brought you into my life, and I'm so grateful for that. You always show up, and that means everything to me.

To Tia Marge—you were the first person I let read this book. You always show up for our family, no matter what. I think the world of you and Uncle Dave, and I'm forever grateful for everything you both do and the love you've given me along the way.

To my ride-or-die BFF, my twin, Jennifer—you are my shield and my sounding board. You've seen every version of me and never flinched. You make my life better just by being in it. Thank you for showing up when I needed you most, and for loving the chaos that comes with me.

To Manders—you are one of my favorite humans and one of my best friends. Thank you not only for being one of my bestest friends, but for being Jax's godmother. That's love on another level, and I'll never take it for granted. I love you!

To my late friend, Becky—you were the spark. You told me I should write a book, and those words stuck with me longer than you probably ever knew. I wish you were here to see this, to crack jokes about edits, or tear up at certain pages. This exists, in part, because of you. And oh yeah... F**K cancer.

To Professor Shelly Spratt, Professor Kristine Carroll, Professor Larissa Favela, Professor Brenda Ahntholz, and every professor who was there along the way at Ohlone College—you all helped me find my voice, my purpose, and my direction. You showed me that I am far smarter than I ever believed possible. Your guidance, your support, and your teaching gave me every tool I needed to actually write and publish this very book.

I said it while I was still sitting under your learning trees, and I'll say it again now: **Ohlone College in Fremont, CA has the best communications program ever.** No debate.

To all teachers—you do the greatest job on Earth and still don't get the pay or recognition you deserve. You show up. You inspire. You lift entire futures. This one's for you.

To the moms, especially in honor of the late, great Willie Brown—who never missed the chance to wish moms a Happy Mother's Day during the Raiders' second-round draft pick—thank you. Your love is the real MVP.

To my mom, Karen—you may not have given birth to me, but you are the mom who raised me. I know I was a difficult teenager, but you kept loving me even when you didn't have to. I'll never forget the time I ran away and you, in heels, still went searching for me in the creek after I kicked your paper under the car. That's the kind of love that stays with a person. I love you, Mom. And I've never stopped doing my all to make you proud.

To the fathers across the NFL who took their sons to games and passed down loyalty like a sacred heirloom—this is for you. We don't just raise fans. We build traditions, legacies, and lifelong bonds.

To Beto, Moi, and the rest of the squad—those Raider Sundays with you crazy nuttys are still some of the best memories of my life. From the tailgates to the chaos to the trash talk, it was pure love. I miss those mornings with all my heart.

To Autumn—I know you ride or die for the Niners, so this marks *one of only four* times in this book I'll give flowers to someone wearing red and gold. But this shoutout goes far beyond football. You are one of the most special and amazing people I've ever known. A dedicated, incredible mom, and one of the best friends a ridiculous guy like me could ever ask for. You've stood by me through some of the roughest times in my life. When I was down on my luck, you didn't just check in—you kept me sane. Your strength, your kindness, your loyalty... I can't thank you enough. I love you, and I adore you. You're family to me.

To Ricky Borba and Cindy Velasco—I've been friends with both of you since the 7th grade. In a world full of random acquaintances, I'm proud and honored to call you true friends. Ricky, reading your book (*Trusting God: Pursuing Your Dreams and Never, Ever Giving Up,* available at your favorite bookseller... had to plug you there, bro!) gave me the extra push to finally do this. And Cindy, your presence in my life has always been steady, kind, and real. I know where your allegiances lie, but we're living proof that a Raider and a Niner can be lifelong friends.

And the forth—and final—shoutout to a Niners fan goes to my brother from another mother, Jarrett. Saucy, we did it. The irony of you being thanked in a Raider book ain't lost on me. But it's the perfect time to say: the darkness is spreading. On a serious note, your long-standing career as a United States Marine and the way you've served this country with honor makes me proud beyond words. I thank you—and all service members—for your sacrifice. And yes, one more time... F**k yo couch.

And finally, to Raider Nation—this is for you. You are the wildest, craziest, most emotionally unbalanced group of extended family members I could've ever asked for... and I wouldn't have it any other way.

Sergio Serna is a proud son of Raider Nation. He's a storyteller, a lifelong fan, and a voice for the culture that shaped him. Born in the Midwest and raised in the heart of the Bay, his journey from outsider to insider mirrors the arc of the very team he loves. Underdog beginnings. Loyal roots. A commitment to never back down.

Sergio is a communications professional, podcast creator, and relentless Raider evangelist. In 2002 and 2003, he covered the team for his college newspaper during their final Super Bowl run. It was a full-circle moment for a kid who grew up repping the Shield like armor. From the BART lots of Oakland to the glimmer of Allegiant Stadium, he's lived the Silver and Black experience with his boots on the pavement and his voice in the mix.

When he's not writing, he's raising his kids (who already bleed Silver and Black), supporting his educator wife Rachel, and finding new ways to honor the past while fighting for the future. He's the founder of Joker and the Queen Publishing and a firm believer that loyalty looks best in black.

One Nation: The Untold Story of Raider Nation is Sergio's way of giving back to the people who gave him belonging, brotherhood, and belief. In his world, Raider Nation isn't something you cheer for. It's something you *live*.

Follow Sergio on X @KingSergioS or visit pulsepodcast.com for more.

To the Raiders organization—

Thank you for building the foundation that birthed a Nation.

Through every city, every era, and every fourth-down heartbreak, you gave us something bigger than football. You gave us identity. You gave us purpose. You gave us the silver and black.

This book is for the fans, but it exists because you lit the fire.

With loyalty, history, and heart,

—On behalf of all of Raider Nation

www.ingramcontent.com/pod-product-compliance
Lightning Source LLC
Chambersburg PA
CBHW051636120626
46551CB00014B/2099